CW00566262

The
GOLDEN AGE
of the
GARDEN

The

GOLDEN
AGE

of the

GARDEN

A MISCELLANY

Edited by
CLAIRE
COCK-STARKEY

First published 2017 by
Elliott and Thompson Limited
27 John Street, London WC1N 2BX
www.eandtbooks.com

ISBN: 978-1-78396-320-1

Picture credits:
Page 68: archivist 2015 / Alamy Stock Photo; page 143: Chronicle /
Alamy Stock Photo; page 162: Mary Evans Picture Library / Alamy
Stock Photo; page 191: archivist 2015 / Alamy Stock Photo; page 252:
archivist 2015 / Alamy Stock Photo.
All other illustrations from *An Encyclopedia of Gardening* by J. C. Loudon, 1822.

9 8 7 6 5 4 3 2 1

A catalogue record for this book is available from the British Library.

Typesetting by Marie Doherty
Printed in the UK by TJ International Ltd

INTRODUCTION

As the seventeenth century made way for the eighteenth, a small revolution in gardening was afoot, one that would change the very nature of great English parks and gardens, and which we continue to appreciate to this day.

During the Renaissance period, the English garden was formal, characterised by trim parterres, elaborate geometric hedges and ordered flower beds, influenced by the Italian and French style of gardens, such as those at Villa d'Este, near Tivoli and at Versailles. But during the seventeenth century, the rigid formality of the previous era gradually started to make way for a more natural method of gardening. Designers and architects began to transform country houses and grounds using nature as their guide and inspiration, devising looser, more sympathetic creations that often featured a body of water to provide picturesque reflections, sweeping views, groves of trees and meandering paths: a landscape inspired by a pastoral ideal.

One of the key early gardens was at Stowe in Buckinghamshire. Initially designed in the formal style, the gardens were adapted and improved by William Kent in the 1730s. Kent introduced a naturalistic style, for example remodelling the formerly octagonal lake into a more organic shape, in order to create a garden that allowed visitors to wander through the park, constantly surprised and delighted by new vistas and architectural features.

As the new movement grew, a name was coined to describe its pioneers: landscape gardener. It was first used in the mid-eighteenth century by poet and gardener William Shenstone and was later adopted by Humphry Repton to describe his profession.

The golden age of English gardens is best encapsulated by the influential designs of Lancelot 'Capability' Brown, a man who used the sunken fence (or ha-ha) to open up the views from the house, looking through the garden to the fields and landscape beyond. His naturalistic planting of clumps, belts and serpentine walks proved extremely popular, and he inspired many imitators.

Brown and his followers were not the only major influence on the English garden of the period, however. Some other key designers were preoccupied with ideas about the nature of beauty and how this translated to the landscape. Most notably William Gilpin, Uvedale Price and Richard Payne Knight pondered on the idea of the 'picturesque' – the creation of a scene that invites the landscape painter to capture it. Price was critical of Brown, finding his landscapes too mannered and formulaic, and argued that for a truly picturesque scene there should be drama in the shape of a gnarled tree, a rugged valley or a rock-strewn cascade.

As the intellectual debate rumbled on, many practical gardeners took the theories of the picturesque and applied them to their designs. Thomas Whately's influential book *Observations on Modern Gardening* (1770) included descriptions of many of the grounds that had been landscaped in this new style. Whately's book proved extremely popular and was instrumental in spreading the English style of garden to the Continent and beyond. Indeed, in 1786 future US presidents Thomas Jefferson and John Adams came to England armed with Whately's tome as their guide as they made a tour through English gardens – a trip that was to prove influential on their own taste in gardening.

As the 'English Garden' took on its own distinct style, it continued to attract fans around the world. Russian Empress Catherine the Great showed much enthusiasm and went on to create two gardens in the English style near St Petersburg. French philosopher Jean-Jacques Rousseau was equally charmed by landscape gardening, and was especially fond of the English-style garden at Ermenonville, near Oise, which had been inspired by Rousseau's writings on the ideal, natural garden.

The reform in the style of English gardening went beyond practical theories and essays on the nature of beauty; it seeped into literature and popular culture. Poets and writers were inspired by the new style – the poet William Shenstone not only wrote about the natural landscape in both verse and prose, he also applied those ideas in his own influential garden, The Leasowes. Writers such as Walter Scott and Daniel Defoe, essayists Joseph Addison and Richard Steele all added their voices to the debate as around them the English national landscape was forever changed by Kent, Brown, Repton and Loudon, among others.

The English garden was not created by one individual but rather by many different voices and practitioners developing and refining the concepts. As time moved on, so new gardeners came to the fore, each adding their own spin to the landscape garden. Unlike Capability Brown and William Kent, who left little in the way of writings on their theories and methods, Humphry Repton and J. C. Loudon both wrote widely on gardening, providing greater understanding of the thinking behind their designs and commentary on those who came before them. Loudon in particular was a keen writer and many of his works, notably *The Gardener's Magazine* and *The Suburban Gardener and Villa Companion* helped translate landscape gardening theories for the smaller gardens of the growing middle classes.

By the early nineteenth century the golden era of garden design was coming to a close as Victorian fashions, such as the wild garden, started to become more popular. J. C. Loudon in a sense embodies the shift from the landscape garden movement towards the Victorian style, which was influenced by the exotic plants coming into Britain from across the Empire and characterised by grand public spaces such as Kew Gardens.

Despite the new trends and fashions in gardening that have come and gone since, many of the creations of that period stand today (Stowe, Blenheim and Chatsworth, for example, retain much of the landscaping from this period), and continue to attract visitors from around the world. *The Golden Age of the Garden* celebrates the era of landscape gardening, looking back on contemporary accounts of its development using letters, essays, diaries, travelogues and gardening manuals. The words of key gardeners, and thinkers, along with descriptions of renowned gardens are interwoven with gardening advice and instruction, providing a fascinating path through the changing themes and styles of the landscape gardening movement.

The novice to the most green-fingered of gardeners will, I hope, find plenty to surprise, inspire and delight within these pages.

*

A note: The archaic spelling and punctuation of the original extracts have been preserved in order to better reflect the writing of the period. Although the golden age of gardens could loosely be defined as coming to a close by the 1840s, I have retained a few extracts from later dates that offer good illustrations of famous golden era gardens or techniques.

Walpole on the perfection of English gardens:

'We have discovered the point of perfection. We have given the true model of gardening to the world; let other countries mimic or corrupt our taste; but let it reign here on its verdant throne, original by its elegant simplicity, and proud of no other art than that of softening nature's harshnesses and copying her graceful touch.'

– *The History of the Modern Taste in Gardening*
by Horace Walpole (1780)

On the joy of the English garden:

Stephen Switzer (1682–1745) was one of the early proponents of landscape gardening. He worked on the gardens of Blenheim, Stowe and Castle Howard, among others, and wrote widely on garden design. His use of meandering serpentine paths through the medieval woodland of Castle Howard's Ray Wood (from 1706) led to a series of clearings in which fountains, seats and statues were artfully placed. It was the first such design of its kind and this move away from the formal planting and geometric designs of the preceding era was hugely influential on the burgeoning art of landscape gardening.

"Tis certain no Nation in the World is blest with more natural Conveniences than we are: The Atheist has no reason to argue against the Hills or other Excrescencies of the Earth as a Blemish of the Creation, since 'tis from them we have those Springs that refresh the Valleys, and the Beauty of which adds such a Magnificence to our Gardens, and such as few Countries (especially those adjoining to us) enjoy so well as ourselves.

'Tis true, we do not abound so much as they do with Oranges, and some other delicious Fruits, but in their room we have more durable and serviceable Blessings of Oak, besides fructiferous Trees, proper enough for our Use, and that which abundantly commands them all, I mean our ships and the Balance of Trade.

If our Seasons are something more uncertain than they are in other Countries, we have no occasion to repine, since the general Temperature of our Climate makes sufficient amends; and that Royal Person aforementioned has worthily observ'd, *We can no longer and better enjoy our Gardens then they can either in the more frigid or torrid Clime.'*

> — *The Nobleman, Gentleman, and Gardener's Recreation*
> by Stephen Switzer (1715)

Rousseau on the perfect garden:

Jean Jacques Rousseau (1712–78) was a French philosopher who, influenced by the writing of his contemporaries such as Joseph Addison, wrote about English gardens and his love of nature, most notably in *Julie, or the New Heloise* (1761). Rousseau spent the last year of his life staying in a cottage in the garden of René de Girardin, who in 1762 had created an extensive park and gardens at Ermenonville, France, in the English style. Rousseau loved the gardens there, and when he died in 1778 was buried on an island in the park, which was renamed in his honour.

'This place [Elysium] is enchanting, it is true, but rustic and wild; I see no human labour here. You closed the gate; water came along I know not how; nature alone did the rest and you yourself could never have managed to do as well ... although I did not find exotic plants and products of the Indies, I found the local ones arranged and combined in a manner that yielded a cheerier and pleasanter effect .... A thousand wild flowers shone there, among which the eye was surprised to detect a few garden varieties .... I saw here and there without order or

Early crimson chrysanthemum.

17

symmetry underbrush of rose, raspberry, and currant bushes, patches of lilac, hazel, elderberry, mock orange, broom, trifolium . . ..'

> – Jean-Jacques Rousseau, 1761 (Philip Stewart and
> Jean Vaché (trans.) 'Julie, or the New Heloise' in The
> collected writings of Rousseau, vol. 6 [Hanover, NH:
> University Press of New England, 1997], pp. 388–389)

On what makes a good gardener:

'The requisite Qualifications of a good Gardener are such as these, *viz.* He should be a middle-aged Man, vigorous and active, one of Experience and large Capacity, diligent, honest, and good-natured, which are Qualifications necessary for every Person.'

> – *The Gentleman's, Traveller's, Husbandman's and
> Gardener's Pocket Companion* (1751)

On the importance of gardening:

Thomas Whately (1726–72) was an English politician who, in 1770, published one of the most important and influential books of the English landscape design era, *Observations on Modern Gardening*.

'Gardening, is the perfection to which it has been lately brought in England, is entitled to a place of considerable rank among the liberal arts. It is as superior to landskip [landscape] painting, as a reality to a representation: it is an exertion of fancy, a subject for taste; and being released now from the restraints of regularity, and enlarged beyond purposes of domestic convenience, the most beautiful, the most simple, the most noble scenes of nature are all within its province: for it is no longer confined to spots from which it borrows its name, but regulates also the disposition and embellishments of a park, a farm, or a riding; and the business of a gardener is to select and to apply whatever is great, elegant, or characteristic in any of them; to discover and to shew all the advantages of the place upon which he is employed; to supply its defects, to correct its faults, and to improve its beauties. For all these operations, the objects of nature are still his only materials.'

— *Observations on Modern Gardening*
by Thomas Whately (1770)

Price on the changing fashions in gardening:

Uvedale Price (1747–1829) was a wealthy landowner, amateur landscape gardener and arbiter of taste. He particularly promoted the theory of the 'picturesque', in which the design of landscape should highlight and improve on nature, reflecting the beauty of landscape paintings.

'Formerly, every thing was in squares and parallelograms; now every thing is in segments of circles, and ellipses: the formality still remains; the character of that formality alone has changed. The old canal, for instance, has lost, indeed, its straitness and its angles; but it is become regularly serpentine, and the edges remain naked, and as uniform as before: avenues, vistas, and strait ridings through woods, are exchanged for clumps, belts and circular roads and plantations of every kind: strait alleys in gardens, and the platform of the old

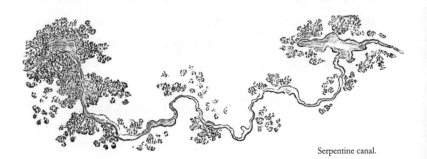

Serpentine canal.

terrace, for the curves of the gravel walk. The intention of the new improvers was certainly meritorious; for they meant to banish formality, and to restore nature; but it must be remembered, that strongly marked, distinct, and regular curves, unbroken and undisguised, are hardly less natural or formal, though much less grand and simple, than strait lines; and that, independently of monotony, the continual and indiscriminate use of such curves, has an appearance of affectation and of studied grace that always creates disgust.'

– *An Essay on the Picturesque* by Uvedale Price, 1796

Moving on from the formal garden:

'Gardening is one of the first arts that stands recorded in the annals of the world! It ever afforded the most rational and pleasing relaxation, and men of sense thirst after its improvements . . ..

It is not above seventy years since Evergreens, Box, and Yew Hedges, cut and pruned into animals and various strange forms, were the wonder of Britain, as they still are, and, for good reasons, must continue to be of Sweden, and other Northern countries.

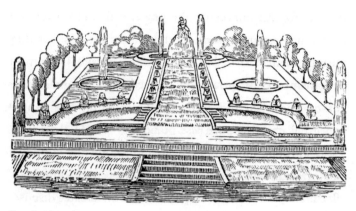

Formal garden style.

The approach to every house of consequence was, at the time alluded to, by a range of small gardens, composed of gravel-walks, with grass-plots or flower-borders on the sides; each little garden rising above the other, (generally by steps) and divided by walls and iron gates; and it was much later than the above date, before such barbarisms began to subside, and make way for true and natural elegance . . ..

By keeping within our eye the propriety and beauties of landscape, we shall alike avoid the geometrical formalities of the old, and the strange and irregular whims of the Chinese garden at this day.

In this Island we now seem to have discovered, and to hold up to others, the TRUE MODEL OF GARDENING. LET OTHER COUNTRIES MIMIC TASTE, AS THEY MIMIC LIBERTY!! But here, by softening the rigours of Nature, and minutely attending to her delightful traits, let Britain reign triumphant IN SIMPLE GRACEFUL ELEGANCE.

Every piece of ground has some variation from another; and of course the natural disposition of each should have particular attention paid to it in making improvements. Its small or striking incidents may then be easily turned to advantage, and a disagreeable sameness be always avoided . . ..

Should no relapse to formality again take place, how gay and charming will each hill and vale appear! The bright example of the man of taste and fortune, will be found to have its due operation on the mind of the enlightened yeoman, and by degrees give suited elegance to the farm and hamlet.'
– *An Essay upon Gardening* by Richard Steele (1800)

General principles of ornamental gardening:

'ARTS merely imitative have but one principle to work by, the *nature* or actual state of the thing to be imitated. In works of design and invention, another principle takes the lead, which is *taste*. And in every work in which mental gratification is not the only object, a third principle arises, utility, or the concomitant purpose for which the production is intended.

The art of *Gardening* is subject to these three principles: to nature, as being an imitative art; to utility, as being productive of objects which are useful as well as ornamental; and to taste, in the choice of fit objects to be imitated, and of fit purposes to be pursued, as also in the composition of the several objects and ends proposed, so as to produce the degree of gratification and use best suited to the *place* and to the *purpose* for which it is about to be ornamented: thus, a Hunting-Box and a Summer Villa,—an Ornamental Cottage and a Mansion, require a different *style* of ornament.'

– *Planting and Ornamental Gardening; A Practical Treatise*
by William Marshall (1785)

Walpole on Kent and his contribution to the natural English garden:

Horace Walpole (1717–97) was the son of Sir Robert Walpole, Britain's first Whig prime minister. Walpole was a politician, intellectual and writer – he believed in constant progress and the superiority of all things English and thus was an advocate of English landscape gardening, keen to trace its history and tie the natural beauty of modern English gardens back to literature (Pope, Milton *et al*). Walpole saw

William Kent as the trailblazer of the movement (although arguably many others were equally important, notably Stephen Switzer and Charles Bridgman).

'But of all the beauties he [William Kent] added to the face of this beautiful country, none surpassed his management of water. Adieu to canals, circular basons, and cascades tumbling down marble steps, that last absurd magnificence of Italian and French villas. The forced elevation of cataracts was no more. The gentle stream taught to serpentize seemingly at its pleasure, and where discontinued by different levels, its course appeared to be concealed by thickets properly interspersed, and glittered again at a distance where it might be supposed naturally to arrive. Its borders were smoothed, but preserved their waving irregularity. A few trees scattered here and there on its edges sprinkled the tame bank that accompanied its meanders; and when it disappeared among the hills, shades descending from the heights leaned towards its progress, and framed the distant point of light under which it was lost, as it turned aside to either hand of the blue horizon.'

— The History of the Modern Taste in Gardening
by Horace Walpole (1780)

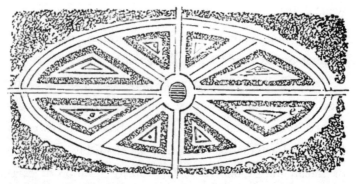

A sample layout for a flower garden.

Catherine the Great on English gardens:

Catherine the Great, Empress of Russia, was highly intelligent and widely read. She was a great admirer of English gardens and had two gardens created in the English style, Tsarskoe Selo and Pavlosk, both near St Petersburg. She wrote to Voltaire on the topic in 1772:

'I am madly in love with English gardens, with curved lines, soft slopes, ponds resembling lakes, firm land archipelagos and I profoundly despise straight lines and paired paths. I hate fountains, which torture water in order to turn its course against nature; statues are put away onto galleries, entrance halls, and so on; in a word, Anglomania rules over my plantomania.'

– Extract from a letter from Catherine the Great
to Voltaire, 25 June (old-style date), 1772

A taste for gardening:

John Claudius Loudon (1783–1843) was one of the last landscape gardeners of the golden era; he formed a bridge between the landscape design movement and the subsequent Victorian fashion of exotic and bright bedding plants. Both Loudon and his wife, Jane Webb Loudon, wrote widely on gardens and gardening, and helped to bring a passion for gardening to the smaller gardens of the burgeoning middle classes.

'The agreeableness and utility of gardening pursuits are so generally known and acknowledged, that it would be superfluous to insist on them here. Horticulture, as a means of subsistence, is one of the first arts attempted by man on emerging from barbarism; and landscape gardening, as an art of design, is one of the latest inventions for the display of wealth and taste in ages of luxury and refinement. The love of gardening is so natural to man, as to be common to children, and the enjoyment of a garden so congenial to our ideas of happiness, as to be desired by men of all ranks and professions, who toil hard in cities, hoping, with Cowley[*],

---

[*] Abraham Cowley (1618–67) was an English poet, who famously wrote 'May I a small house and large garden have; And a few friends, And many books, both true.'

one day to retire to "a small house and a large garden." The cares of a garden are a source of agreeable domestic recreation, and especially to the female sex; to the valetudinarian they are a source of health, and to age a source of interest; for it has been remarked of a taste for gardening, that, unlike other tastes, it remains with us to the latest period, and increases rather than diminishes.'

– *The Gardener's Magazine* by J. C. Loudon (1826)

On the disposition of a garden:

'The End and Design of a good Garden, is to be both profitable and delightful; wherein should be observed, that its Parts should always be presenting new Objects, which is a continual Entertainment to the Eye, and raises a Pleasure of Imagination.'

– *New Principles of Gardening* by Batty Langley (1728)

In praise of gardening:

'With so many happy Circumstances is the Exercise of *Gardening* attended, that greater Encomiums [praise] can scarcely be given to any other: But of them all, I shall only mention, and that briefly, these following:

1. The *Delightfulness*,
2. The *Innocency*,
3. The *Healthfulness*,
4. The *Advantageousness*;

And,

5. The *Honorableness*.

1. As to the first, What can be more *Delightful,* than in the *Spring-time*, to behold the Infant Plants putting forth their verdant Heads, from the Bosom of their fostering Mother Earth? In the *Summer Months*, the Flowers ting'd with a Variety of the most charming Dyes, seeming, as it were, to vie with each other, which shall most allure the Beholder's Eye with their splendid Gaiety, and entertain the Nostrils with their enlivening Fragrancy? And in *Autumn*, to views the bending Boughs, as it were, submissively offering their delicious Fruit, and courting the Gatherer's Acceptance?

2. As for *Innocency*; Horticulture was by the All-wife Creator appointed to be the Employment of our first Parents in

29

their innocent State. And what Employment can be more harmless? No Cruelty is used in this Exercise, unless the destroying of noxious vermin that prey upon and devour the blessed Products of the Earth, can merit opprobrious Name. What though the skilful Pruner scarifies bark-bound Trees, and displaces the barren, useless, and too luxuriant Branches, that rob the healthful and more useful parts of their due Nourishment? These Wounds cause no Sense of Pain to the tenderest Plants; they heal up without Dressing or Bandage, and are thereby reduced to a more regular Beauty, a more healthful Constitution, and to a greater Fertility.

3. It is *Healthful.* It is true, since the Fall of our Progenitors, the Work is not so easy as before it was; the Curse having covered the Ground Work is not so easy as before it was; the Curse having covered the ground with *Thorns* and *Briars*, and caused unprofitable Weeds to spring up among the useful Plants, to rob them of their proper Nourishment; so that the Ground which before, without Cultivation, would have been spontaneously obedient to vegetative Nature, must now, by the Sweat of the Brow, and no little Labour, be brought under Subjection: But then at the same time, to make Amends, this very Labour is salutiferous: The Exercise of the Body prevents the Blood and Juices from stagnating and growing corrupt; and the Labourer is every Moment drawing in with his Breath a wholesome

and enlivening Stream from the Earth, which heighten'd with the spicy Fragrancy of odoriferous Plants, causes the Blood and Spirits to circulate briskly; and together with the Motion of the Body, forces out and expels the morbid Parts through the Pores, which exhaling, leaves what remains more pure and uncontaminated. Besides, Labour sets an Edge to the Appetite, gives a more grateful and delicious Relish to the Products of the Earth, and at Night disposes the whole bodily Frame into a Capacity for the full Enjoyment of those refreshing Slumbers, that balmy Sleep, which generally forsakes the Downy Couches of the inactive, indolent Great.

4. That it is *Advantageous*, no one will dispute, who sees, with what mighty Returns, even more than an hundred-fold, a diligent and skilful Culture repays the Labours of the sedulous Cultivator, producing an innocent and wholesome Food, that bountifully supplies to himself all the Necessaries of Life, and administers to all around him, of what Condition or Quality soever, sufficient to adorn the Table, and serve for Use and Elegance.

5. The Exercise is *Honourable*. For had it not the Great God himself for its first Artist, who not only laid out a Plan of the *Garden of Eden*, but is also said to have planted it with a vast Variety of the most beautiful Trees, Plants and Flowers? And the Cultivating of it was appointed to be the Business of

the Sole Monarch and Lord of this terrestrial Globe, by his Creator, who in his great Wisdom found no Occupation so suitable as this, to that Innocence and Perfection of Nature in which he had form'd the first Man; who before the Fall, could enjoy no Earthly Delight equal to a Garden exquisitely adorn'd with Trees and Plants, every where embellish'd with beautiful Flowers, and shining with grateful Fruits, abounding with wholesome Springs and crystal Rivers, echoing with the melodious Harmony of the winged Choristers, and crown'd with a temperate Air, and a charming Vicissitude of kindly Seasons.'

— *The Gardeners Dictionary* by Philip Miller (1737)

On Stowe:

Stowe in Oxfordshire is one of the foremost examples of Georgian gardening. The gardens were redeveloped from 1713 by Viscount Cobham, who commissioned garden designer Charles Bridgeman and architect Sir John Vanbrugh to carry out the works. Viscount Cobham continued to make improvements, frequently consulting with the celebrated designers of the day, including William Kent and Capability Brown.

'BUCKINGHAM Town you pass through a little Village called CHATMORE, and from thence to the NEW INN at the South Entrance at the Garden called STOW [*sic*]. This is a Prospect that agreeably surprises you; for, upon quitting an unpleasant Road, you perceive all at once a long Avenue; at the End of which rises a fine View of my Lord's House, through a double Row of Arbail-Trees. This charming Garden you enter by a Slope that leads to a superb Terras, which is carried cross-ways the whole Weadth of the Ground, that lays parallel before you.

. . .

From thence you descend to a large Piece of Water. At a Distance we behold two beautiful Rivers, which join, an irregular Bason in one Stream, which falls into the Lake and makes a Cascade. Here is such a scene of Magnificence and Nature display'd at one View. To the Right you have a View of the *Gothic* Temple, Lord COBHAM's Pillar, and

A waterfall or cascade.

the Bridge; in the Center is a grand View of the House, and on the Left the Piramid; the Trees and Water so delightfully intermingled, and such charming Verdure, symmetry, and Proportion every where presenting to the Eye, that the Judgment is agreeably puzzled, which singularly to prefer, of so many Beauties.'

– *The Beauties of Stow* by George Bickham (1753)

Price on the English tradition of laying out gardens:

'There is no country, I believe (if we except China) where the art of laying our grounds is so much cultivated as it is now in England. Formerly the decorations near the house were infinitely more magnificent and expensive than they are at present; but the embellishments of what are called grounds, and of all the extensive scenery round the place, was much less attended to; and, in general, the park, with all its timber, was left in a state of wealthy neglect: as these embellishments are now extended over a whole district, and as they give a new and peculiar character to the general face of the country, it is well worth considering whether they give a natural and a beautiful one, and whether the present system of improving (to use a short though often an inaccurate term) is founded on any just principles of taste.'

– An Essay on the Picturesque by Uvedale Price, 1796

Scott on the English garden:

Writer Walter Scott became increasingly interested in gardens after he bought his Scottish manor house, Abbotsford, in 1811, and began to remodel the grounds. So interested was he in the differing schools of thought on the proper way to lay out country estates, his thoughts began to seep into his work, and here in the preface to his historical novel *Quentin Durward*, he ponders on the fashion for simplicity:

'Its remains run along a beautiful terrace over-hanging the river Loire, which had been formerly laid out with a succession of flights of steps, highly ornamented with statues, rock-work, and other artificial embellishments, descending from one terrace to another, until the very verge of the river was attained. All this architectural decoration, with its accompanying parterres of rich flowers and exotic shrubs, had, many years since, given place to the more profitable scene of the vine-dresser's labours; yet the remains, too massive to be destroyed, are still visible, and, with the various artificial slopes and levels of the high bank, bear perfect evidence how actively Art had been here employed to decorate Nature.

Few of these scenes are now left in perfection; for the fickleness of fashion has accomplished in England the total change which devastation and popular fury have produced in the French pleasure-grounds. For my part, I am contended to subscribe to the opinion of the best qualified judge of our time [Scott is here referring to Uvedale Price], who thinks we have carried to an extreme our taste for simplicity, and that the neighbourhood of a stately mansion requires some more ornate embellishments than can be derived from the meagre accompaniments of grass and gravel. A highly romantic situation may be degraded, perhaps by an attempt at such artificial ornaments; but then, in by far the greater number of sites, the intervention of more architectural decoration than is now in use, seems necessary to redeem the naked tameness of a large house placed by itself in the midst of a lawn, where it looks as much unconnected with all around as if it had walked out of town upon an airing.

How the taste came to change so suddenly and absolutely, is rather a singular circumstance, unless we explain it on the same principle on which the three friends

Architectural decorations; a rustic hut.

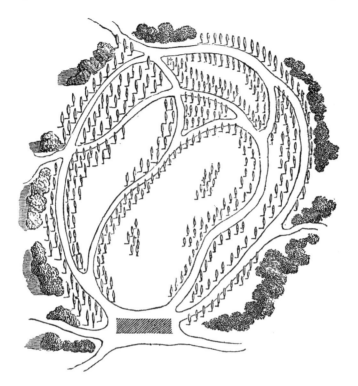

A *ferme ornée.*

of the father in Molière's comedy recommend a cure for the melancholy of his daughter – that he should furnish her apartment, namely, with paintings – with tapestry – or with china, according to the different commodities in which each of them was a dealer. Tried by this scale, we may perhaps discover that, of old, the architect laid out the garden and the pleasure-grounds in the neighbourhood of the mansion, and, naturally enough, displayed his own art there in statues and vases, and paved terraces and flights of steps, with ornamented balustrades; while the gardener, subordinate in rank, endeavoured to make the vegetable kingdom correspond to the prevailing taste, and cut his evergreens into verdant walls, with towers and battlements, and his detached trees into a resemblance of statuary. But the wheel has since revolved, so as to place the landscape gardener, as he is called, almost upon a level with the architect; and hence a liberal and somewhat violent use is made of spade and pick-axe, and a conversion of the ostentatious labours of the architect into a *ferme ornée**, as little different from the simplicity of Nature, as displayed in the surrounding country, as the comforts of convenient and cleanly walks, imperiously demanded in the vicinage of a gentleman's residence, can possibly admit.'

– Preface to *Quentin Durward* by Walter Scott (1823)

On garden composition:

'Nature, always simple, employs but four materials in the composition of her scenes, *ground*, *wood*, *water*, and *rocks*.

---

* The term *ferme ornée* literally means ornamented farm and came into use after Stephen Switzer described country estates which were partly designed for function (as farms) and partly for aesthetics, thus.

The cultivation of nature has introduced a fifth species, the *buildings* requisite for the accommodation of men. Each of these again admit of varieties in their figure, dimensions, colour, and situation. Every landskip is composed of these parts only; every beauty in a landskip depends on the application of their several varieties.'

> – *Observations on Modern Gardening*
> by Thomas Whately (1770)

Pope on an idealised English scene:

Alexander Pope (1688–1744) was part of the Augustan poetry movement which harked backed to Classical times. However his poetry which frequently touched on the landscape and his scathing satire which poured scorn on the formal gardens of the French and Dutch, was very influential on William Kent and Joseph Addison, and as such he is seen as an inspiration to the burgeoning landscape garden movement.

'THY forests, Windsor! and thy green retreats,
At once the Monarch's and the Muses' seats,
Invite my lays. Be present, sylvan maids!

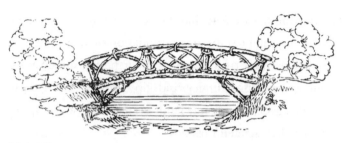

A Swiss bridge.

Unlock your springs, and open all your shades.
Granville commands; your aid, O Muses, bring!
What Muse for Granville can refuse to sing?
The groves of Eden, vanished now so long,
Live in description, and look green in song:
These, were my breast inspired with equal flame,
Like them in beauty, should be like in fame.
Here hills and vales, the woodland and the plain,
Here earth and water seem to strive again;
Not chaoslike together crushed and bruised,
But, as the world, harmoniously confused:
Where order in variety we see,
And where, though all things differ, all agree.
Here waving groves a chequered scene display,
And part admit and part exclude the day;
As some coy nymph her lover's warm address
Nor quite indulges, nor can quite repress.
There, interspersed in lawns and opening glades,

Thin trees arise that shun each other's shades.
Here in full light the russet plains extend:
There, wrapped in clouds the bluish hills ascend:
Ev'n the wild heath displays her purple dyes,
And midst the desert fruitful fields arise,
That crowned with tufted trees and springing corn,
Like verdant isles the sable waste adorn.
Let India boast her plants, nor envy we
The weeping amber or the balmy tree,
While by our oaks the precious loads are borne,
And realms commanded which those trees adorn.'

– 'Windsor Forest' by Alexander Pope (1713)

Repton on the art of landscape gardening:

After an unsuccessful start in business, Humphry Repton (1752–1818) decided to follow his passion and embark on a career as a landscape gardener. Repton very much advanced the landscape gardening movement through both his designs and his writing on the subject and was seen as the worthy successor of Capability Brown. Repton's most famous works include Sheringham Park, Woburn Abbey and Cobham Hall.

'The Art of Landscape Gardening (which more peculiarly belongs to this country) is the only Art which every one professes to understand, and even to practise, without having studied its Rudiments. No man supposes he can paint a Landscape, or play an instrument, without some knowledge of Painting and Music; but every one thinks himself competent to lay out grounds, and sometimes to plan a House for himself, or to criticise on what others propose, without having bestowed a thought on the first principles of *Landscape Gardening* or *Architecture*.

That the two Sister Arts are, and must be inseparable, is obvious from the following consideration. The most beautiful scenes in Nature may surprize at first sight, or delight for a time, but they cannot long be interesting, unless made habitable; therefore, the whole Art of Landscape Gardening may properly be defined, *The pleasing combination of Art and Nature adapted to the use of Man.*'

– *Fragments on the Theory and Practice of Landscape Gardening*
by Humphry Repton (1816)

Gilpin on art and landscape:

William Gilpin (1724–1804) was a cleric and artist who rose to prominence as a travel writer after he published a number of works on his tours of Britain. Gilpin was an adherent to the idea of the 'picturesque', reflecting on nature in terms of how it may be portrayed in art, which were later built on and related to landscape gardening by Uvedale Price and Richard Payne Knight.

'A house is an *artificial* object; and the scenery around it, *must*, in some degree, partake of *art*. Propriety requires it: convenience demands it. But if it partake of *art*, as allied to the *mansion*; it should also partake of *nature*, as allied to the *country*. It has therefore two characters to support; and may be considered as the connecting thread between the regularity of the house, and the freedom of the natural scene. These two characters it should ever have in view.'

– Observations on the Mountains and Lakes of Cumberland and Westmoreland by William Gilpin (1786)

Price's definition of picturesque:

'There are few words whose meaning has been less accurately determined than that of the word Picturesque.

In general, I believe, it is applied to every object, and every kind of scenery, which has been, or might be represented with good effect in painting; just as the word beautiful (when we speak of visible nature) is applied to every object, and every kind of scenery, that in any way give pleasure to the eye; and these seem to be the significations of both words, taken in their most extended and popular sense.'

– *An Essay on the Picturesque* by Uvedale Price, 1796

The Landskip:

'How pleas'd within my native bowers
Ere while I pass'd the day!
Was ever scene so deck'd with flowers?
Were ever flowers so gay?

How sweetly smil'd the hill, the vale,
And all the landskip round!
The river gliding down the dale!
The hill with beeches crown'd!

But now, when urg'd by tender woes
I speed to meet my dear,

That hill and stream my zeal oppose,
And check my fond career.

No more, since DAPHNE was my theme,
Their wonted charms I see:
That verdant hill, and silver stream,
Divide my love and me.'

– *The Works in Verse and Prose of
William Shenstone* (1777, 5th ed.)

Whately on Painshill:

The gardens at Painshill near Cobham, Surrey, are a classic example of English landscape gardening in the naturalistic style. The gardens were laid out 1738–73, from the pioneering designs of the Honourable Charles Hamilton who, inspired after a Grand Tour of Europe, wished to create a garden that presented the visitor with a series of beautiful scenes. He was a keen plantsman and imported many new and exotic plants for Painshill, most notably from the famed botanist John Bartram in Pennsylvania, who sent over great boxes of seeds.

'Painshill is situated on the utmost verge of a moor, which rises above a fertile plain, watered by the Mole. Large vallies descending to different directions towards the river, break the brow into separate eminences; and the gardens are extended along the edge, in a semi-circular form, between the winding river which describes their outward boundary, and the park which fills up the cavity of the crescent: the moor lies behind the place, and sometimes appears too conspicuously: but the views on the other sides into the cultivated country are agreeable: they are terminated by hills at a competent distance; the plain is sufficiently varied with objects; and the richest meadows overspread the bottom just below: the prospects are, however, only pretty, not fine; and the river is languid and dull. Painshill therefore, is little benefitted by external circumstances; but the scenes within itself are both grand and beautiful; and the disposition of the gardens affords frequent opportunities of seeing the several parts, the one from the other, across the park, in a variety of advantageous situations.

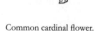

The house stands at one extremity of the crescent, on a hill which is shut out from the park, but open to the country. The view is cheerful; and the spot is laid out in an elegant garden taste, pretending to no more than

Common cardinal flower.

46

to be pleasant. In the midst of the thicket which separates it from the park, is a parterre, and an orangerie, where the exotic plants are, during the summer, intermixed with common shrubs, and a constant succession of flowers. The space before the house is full of ornament; the ground is prettily varied; and several sorts of beautiful trees are disposed on the sides in little open plantations.

This hill is divided from another much larger by a small valley; and on the top of the second eminence, at a seat just above a large vineyard which overspreads all the side, a scene totally different appears: the general prospect, though beautiful, is the circumstance the least engaging; the attention is immediately attracted from the cultivated plain, to the point of a hanging wood at a distance, but still within the place, and which is not only a noble object in itself, but affords the most pleasing encouragement to all who delight in gardening; for it has been raised by the present possessor; and by its situation, its thickness, and extent, while it retains the freshness of a young plantation, has already in appearance all the massy richness of an old one . . ..

But Painshill is all a new creation; and a boldness of design, and a happiness of execution, attend the wonderful efforts which art has there made to rival nature.

. . .

An easy winding descent leads from the Gothic building to the lake, and a broad walk is afterwards continued along the banks, and across an island, close to the water on one hand, and skirted by wood on the other: the spot is perfectly retired; but the retirement is cheerful; the lake is calm; but it is full to the brim, and never darkened with shadow; the walk is smooth, and almost level, and touches the very margin of the water; the wood which secludes all view into the country, is composed of the most elegant trees, full of the lightest greens, and bordered with shrubs and with flowers; and though the place is almost surrounded with plantations, yet within itself is open and airy; it is embellished with three bridges, a ruined arch, and a grotto; and the Gothic building, still very near, and impending directly over the lake, belongs to the place; but these objects are never visible all together; they appear in succession as the walk proceeds; and their number does not croud the scene which is enriched by their frequency.'

— *Observations on Modern Gardening*
by Thomas Whately (1770)

Repton on landscape gardening as compared to ancient gardening:

'The perfection of *Landscape Gardening* consists in the four following requisites:

First, it must display the natural beauties, and hide the natural defects of every situation. *Secondly*, it should give the appearance of extent and freedom, by carefully disguising or hiding the boundary. *Thirdly*, it must studiously conceal every interference of art, however expensive, by which the natural scenery is improved; making the whole appear the production of nature only; and *fourthly*, all objects of mere convenience or comfort, if incapable of being made orna-mental, or of becoming proper parts of the general scenery, must be removed or concealed.

Each of these four objects enumerated are strictly oppo-site to the principles of ancient gardening, which may be

Repton's landscaping at Rivenhall Place.

thus stated: *First*, the natural beauties or defects of a situation had no influence, when it was the fashion to exclude by lofty walls every surrounding object. *Secondly*, these walls were never considered as defects, but, on the contrary, were ornamented with vases, expensive iron gates, and palisades, to render them more conspicuous. *Thirdly*, so far from making gardens appear natural, every expedient was used to display the costly efforts of Art, by which Nature had been subdued: the ground was levelled by a line; the water was squared or rounded into regular basons; the trees, if not clipped into artificial shapes, were at least so planted by line and measurement, that the formal hand of art could no where be mistaken. And, *Fourthly*, with respect to object of convenience, they were placed as near the house as possible: the stables, the barns, and the kitchen garden, were among the ornaments of a place; while the village, the almshouse, the parish school, and church-yard, were not attempted to be concealed by the walls or palisades that divided them from the embellished pleasure-ground.'

– An Enquiry into the Changes of taste in Landscape Gardening
by H. Repton (1806)

Adams on visiting English gardens:

In April 1786, two future US Presidents, John Adams and Thomas Jefferson (Adams was second US President from 1797, Jefferson was third from 1801–1809) toured England together in a hired coach with Thomas Whately's *Observations on Modern Gardening* as their guide. Adams and Jefferson visited a number of gardens, and Adams recorded his thoughts in his diary:

'Mr. Jefferson and myself, went in a Post Chaise to Woburn Farm, Caversham, Wotton, Stowe, Edghill, Stratford upon Avon, Birmingham, the Leasowes, Hagley, Stourbridge, Worcester, Woodstock, Blenheim, Oxford, High Wycomb, and back to Grosvenor Square.'

. . .

'The Gentlemens Seats were the highest Entertainment, We met with. Stowe, Hagley and Blenheim, are superb. Woburn, Caversham and the Leasowes are beautifull. Wotton is both great and elegant tho neglected. Architecture, Painting, Statuary, Poetry are all employed in the Embellishment of these Residences of Greatness and Luxury. A national Debt of 274 millions sterling accumulated by jobs, Contracts, Salaries and Pensions in the Course of a Century might easily produce all this Magnificence. The Pillars, Obelisks &c. erected in honour of Kings, Queens and Princesses, might procure the means. The Temples to Bacchus and Venus, are quite unnecessary as Mankind have no need of artificial Incitements, to such Amuzements. The Temples of ancient Virtue, of the British Worthies, of Friendship, of Concord and Victory, are in a higher Taste. I mounted Ld. Cobhams Pillar 120 feet high, with pleasure, as his Lordships Name was familiar to me, from Popes Works.

Ld. Littletons Seat interested me, from a recollection of his Works, as well as the Grandeur and Beauty of the Scaenes. Popes Pavillion and Thompsons [Thomson's] Seat, made the Excursion poetical. Shenstones Leasowes is the simplest and plainest, but the most rural of all. I saw no Spot so small, that exhibited such a Variety of Beauties.

It will be long, I hope before Ridings, Parks, Pleasure Grounds, Gardens and ornamented Farms grow so much in fashion in America. But Nature has done greater Things and furnished nobler Materials there. The Oceans, Islands, Rivers, Mountains, Valleys are all laid out upon a larger Scale. – If any Man should hereafter arise, to embellish the rugged Grandeur of Pens Hill, he might make some thing to boast of, although there are many Situations capable of better Improvement.'

– Extract from the diary of second US President
John Adams, 4–10 April 1786

Walpole on the history of the garden:

'Gardening was probably one of the first arts that succeeded to that of building houses, and naturally attended property and individual possession. Culinary, and afterwards medicinal herbs, were the objects of every head of a family: it became convenient to have them within reach, without seeking them at random in woods, in meadows and on mountains, as often as they were wanted. When the earth ceased to furnish spontaneously all these primitive luxuries, and culture became requisite, separate inclosures for rearing herbs grew expedient. Fruits were in the same predicament, and those most in use or that demand attention, must have entered into and extended the domestic inclosure. The good man Noah, we are told, planted a vineyard, drank of the wine, and was drunken, and everybody knows the consequences. Thus we acquired kitchen-gardens, orchards and vineyards.'

– *The History of the Modern Taste in Gardening*
by Horace Walpole (1780)

Price on his hopes for English gardening:

'It seems to me, that there is something of patriotism in the praises which Mr. Walpole and Mr. Mason have bestowed on English gardening; and that zeal for the honour of their country, has made them (in the general view of the subject) over-look defects, which they themselves have condemned. My love for my country, is, I trust not less ardent than theirs, but it has taken a different turn; and I feel anxious to free it from the disgrace of propagating a system, which, should it become universal, would disfigure the face of all Europe. I wish a more liberal and extended idea of improvement to prevail; that instead of the narrow, mechanical practice of a few English gardeners – the noble and varied works of eminent painters of every age, and of every country, and those of their supreme mistress, Nature, should be the great models of imitation.'

– *An Essay on the Picturesque* by Uvedale Price, 1796

On landscape gardening:

'But landscape gardening has created in Britain parks and pleasure-grounds unequalled in any other part of the world.

Planting trees to form glades and squares.

These remain as examples of what might still be done; but in laying out new, or improving old residences, there seems to be a great want, either of industry or ability to profit from them. There are, no doubt, exceptions; but there is not a tithe of the country seats laid out within the last thirty years that do not owe their beauty more to the climate and the architect than to the disposition of the woody scenery. Very few country gentlemen have a just feeling for what painters call general effect; breadth of light and shade; connection and grouping of parts; the importance of which is so ably illustrated by Girardin*, Price, and other authors. Many, with every desire to excel, consider that when they have engaged a first-rate gardener, he will do every thing required in laying out or improving a place. But the sort of knowledge required for the disposition of scenery is very different from that

---

* René de Girardin was a French gardener and author of *De la Composition des Paysages* (1777), which reflected the French style of landscape gardening. His work at Ermenonville was the first example of a French landscape garden.

requisite for the culture and management of a garden; and a gardener can no more be expected to possess it, than a mason or carpenter the science and taste of the architect . . ..

It has been objected to landscape gardeners that no two of them agree about the mode of laying out a plan, or the beauties of a verdant scene; but it may be asked, if two of any other art agrees in any thing but on certain fixed or received principles? Will two architects agree in their plans for repairing a house? Or two physicians in prescribing for a patient? It is enough if scientific men and artists agree in the fundamental principles of their art . . .. Hence the great variety of opinions as to the beauties produced by modern landscape gardening, whose principles of composition admit of infinite variety of application in order to imitate nature, compared with the general approbation of the antient style of laying out grounds whose principles were those of regularity or formality, in order to produce works easily recognised as artificial.'

– *The Gardener's Magazine* by J. C. Loudon (1826)

On gardening jobs for January:

'January. Aquarius, or the Water-Bearer

This Month being generally very cold, and the Earth frozen, there is little to be done in Gardening; but you may prepare a Mixture of Earth and Sheep's Dung to rot and mellow together for a considerable Time, to layer your Flowers with; and make ready such Ground as you shall have occasion for, by Trenching, &c. and Dunging that part that wanteth, and be provided with Horse, Neat and Sheep's Dung of two Years old, and with it mingle Loam, and under Pasture fine Mould, and stir them together, and then skreen it, &c. Uncover the Roots of Fruit-trees where there is Occasion, and Transplant such as you have a mind to, and set Quicksets; prune and lop Trees, and gather Scions for grafting before the Buds appear.'

– The Gentleman's, Traveller's, Husbandman's and
Gardener's Pocket Companion (1751)

On the faults of the English garden:

Not everyone admired the fashion for landscape gardening; Sir William Chambers took rather a dim view of the works

Architectural decorations; a Grecian temple.

of William Kent and Capability Brown, who he felt created gardens little better than fields. Chambers preferred the asymmetric, naturalistic gardens of the Chinese, which he praised for including 'scenes of terror' with sunless valleys, ravaged rocks and gnarled trees that delighted the senses.

'At his first entrance, he sees a large green field, scattered over with a few straggling trees, and verged with a confused border of little shrubs and flowers; on farther inspection, he finds a little serpentine path, twining in regular esses amongst the shrubs of the border, upon which he is to go round, to look on one side at what he has already seen, the large green field; and on the other side at the boundary, which is never more than a few yards from him, and always obtruding upon his sight. From time to time he perceives a little seat or temple stuck up against the wall: happy in the discovery, he sits down to rest his wearied limbs, and then reels on again, cursing the line of beauty; till, spent with fatigue, half roasted by the sun, for there is never any shade, and dying for want of entertainment, he resolves to see no more: vain resolution! There is but one path; he must either drag on to the end, or return by the tedious way he came.'

– A Dissertation on Oriental Gardening
by Sir William Chambers (1772)

Addison on nature and art:

The early part of the eighteenth century saw many intellectuals preoccupied with considering the nature of beauty and the relationship between art and landscape. This essay by Joseph Addison (who alongside his friend, Richard Steele established *The Spectator*, a daily publication that lasted from 1711–12) was very influential in the development of the early English landscape garden:

'If we consider the works of nature and art, as they are qualified to entertain the imagination, we shall find the last very defective in comparison of the former; for though they may sometimes appear as beautiful or strange, they can have nothing in them of that vastness and immensity, which afford so great an entertainment to the mind of the beholder. – The one may be as polite and delicate as the other, but can never show herself so august and magnificent in the design. There is something more bold and masterly in the rough careless strokes of nature than in the nice touches and embellishments of art. The beauties of the most stately garden or palace lie in a narrow compass, the imagination immediately runs them over, and requires something else to gratify her; but in the wide fields of nature the sight wanders up and down without confinement, and is fed with an infinite variety of images without any certain stint or number. For this reason we always find the poet in love with a country life, where nature appears in the greatest perfection, and furnishes out all those scenes that are most apt to delight the imagination . . ..

But though there are several of these wild scenes that are more delightful than any artificial shows, yet we find the

works of nature still more pleasant, the more they resemble those of art; for in this case our pleasure rises from a double principle, from the agreeableness of the objects to the eye, and from their similitude to other objects: we are pleased as well with comparing their beauties as with surveying them, and can represent

Wild service.

them to our minds either as copies or originals. Hence it is that we take delight in a prospect which is well laid out, and diversified with fields and meadows, woods and rivers; in those accidental landscapes of trees, clouds, and cities that are sometimes found in the veins of marble; in the curious fretwork of rocks and grottoes; and, in a word, in anything that hath such a variety or regularity as may seem the effect of design in what we call the works of chance.

If the products of nature rise in value according as they more or less resemble those of art, we may be sure that artificial works receive a greater advantage from their resemblance of such as are natural; because here the similitude is not only pleasant, but the pattern more perfect. The prettiest landscape I ever saw, was one drawn on the walls of a dark room, which stood opposite on one side to a navigable river, and on the other to a park. The experiment is very common in optics. Here you might discover the waves and fluctuations of the water in strong and proper colours, with the picture of a ship entering at one end and sailing by degrees through the whole piece. On another there appeared the green shadows of trees, waving to and fro with the wind, and herds of deer among them in miniature, leaping about upon the wall. I must confess, the novelty of such a sight may be one occasion of its pleasantness to the imagination, but certainly the chief reason is its near resemblance to nature, as it does not only, like other pictures, give the colour and figure, but the motion of the things it represents.

We have before observed, that there is generally in nature something more grand and august than what we meet with in the curiosities of art. When, therefore, we see this imitated in any measure, it gives us a nobler and more exalted kind of pleasure than what we receive from the nicer and more accurate productions of art. On this account our English gardens are not so entertaining to the fancy as those in France and Italy, where we see a large extent of ground covered over with an agreeable mixture of garden and for-est, which represent everywhere an artificial rudeness much more charming than that neatness and elegancy which we meet with in those of our own country. It might, indeed, be of ill consequence to the public, as well as unprofitable to private persons, to alienate so much ground from pasturage and the plough in many parts of a country that is so well peopled, and cultivated to a far greater advantage. But why may not a whole estate be thrown into a kind of garden by frequent plantations, that may turn as much to the profit as the pleasure of the owner? A marsh overgrown with wil-lows, or a mountain shaded with oaks, are not only more beautiful, but more beneficial, than when they lie bare and unadorned. Fields of corn make a pleasant prospect, and if the walks were a little taken care of that lie between them, if the natural embroidery of the meadows were helped and improved by some small additions of art, and the several rows of hedges set off by trees and flowers that the soil was capable of receiving, a man might make a pretty landscape of his own possessions.

Writers who have given us an account of China tell us the inhabitants of that country laugh at the plantations of our Europeans, which are laid out by the rule and line; because, they say, any one may place trees in equal rows and uniform figures. They choose rather to show a genius in works of this nature, and therefore always conceal the art by which they direct themselves. They have a word, it seems, in their language, by which they express the particular beauty of a plantation that thus strikes the imagination at first sight, without discovering what it is that has so agreeable an effect. Our British gardeners, on the contrary, instead of humouring nature, love to deviate from it as much as possible. Our trees rise in cones, lobes, and pyramids. We see the marks of the sissors upon every plant and bush. I do not know whether I am singular in my opinion, but, for my own part, I would rather look upon a tree in all its luxuriancy and diffusion of boughs and branches, than when it is thus cut and trimmed into a mathematical figure; and cannot but fancy that an orchard in flower looks infinitely more delightful than all the little labyrinths of the most finished parterre. But as our great modellers of gardens have their magazines of plants to dispose of, it is very natural for them to tear up all the beautiful plantations of fruit trees, and contrive a plan that may most turn to their own profit, in taking off their evergreens and the like moveable plants, with which their shops are plentifully stocked.'

– Joseph Addison essay in
The Spectator (no. 414, 25 June, 1712)

On the best months to visit English gardens:

'Dear Sir, Your request, so politely, and so warmly urged, to give you a particular description of those celebrated scenes, which rise, Envil, and the Leasowes; as well as my opinion on what is most essential in the modern practice of gardening, wholly engages my attention . . .

There are two seasons wherein parks, and pleasure grounds, are most beautiful. – But in my opinion, notwith-standing *October* is to be preferred, for giving to the woods a more pleasing, and picturesque foliage, *May* certainly has another advantage, and perhaps a superior one, in giving a more lovely and exquisite colouring to the lawns; and though at the same time, the woods may not be so extrava-gantly variegated, yet, if we add the pleasure of beholding nature, rising, like youthful beauty, into a glow of perfection;

and not as in the autumnal months, fading with a cheerless, dying languor.'

– Letters on the Beauties of Hagley, Envil, and the Leasowes
by Joseph Heely (1777)

On modern gardens:

'But it is very lately that the truly magnificent Taste in *Gardening* has flourish'd in these Northern Parts of *Europe*; for although in King Charles the Second's Reign, there was a great Spirit amongst the Nobility and Gentry of *England*, for *Planting* and *Gardening*, which Spirit was greatly heighten'd in King William's Reign, during which Time most of the large Gardens in England were laid out and planted; yet we find the Taste at that Time extended little farther than to small Pieces of Box-work, Finish'd Parterres, and Clipp'd Greens, all which are now generally banish'd out of the Gardens of the most polite Persons of this Age, who justly prefer the more extended Rural Designs of Gardens which approach the nearest to Nature.'

– The Gardeners Dictionary by Philip Miller (1737)

Repton on sameness:

'When the straight walks and lofty walls of ancient gardening had disgusted by their sameness, prevailing in all places alike, whether great or small, it was naturally to be expected that fashion would run into the opposite extreme, by making everything curved as the greatest contrast to straight. To the little interest we experience after the first hundred paces, in a meandering walk betwixt two broad verges of grass, at a great distance from the beds of flowers and shrubs, may be added the mistake of mixing together in such a manner every kind of plant, that no one part of the garden differs from another. Yet there are many pleasure-grounds of this kind, with walks of a tedious length, which I have shuddered to encounter: for this reason I have never advised such walks, except as connecting lines leading to other objects.'

– Fragments on the Theory and Practice of Landscape Gardening
by Humphry Repton (1816)

On the Leasowes:

The Leasowes in Dudley, West Midlands, was created by the poet William Shenstone between 1743 and 1763 and is an early example of the natural style of English landscape gardening. The grounds started life as a farm and Shenstone gradually added more ornamentation and planting to evoke pastoral scenes described in the poetry he enjoyed, ultimately creating a *ferme ornée*.

'The Leasowes is situate [sic] in the parish of Hales Owen, a small market town, in the county of Salop; but surrounded by other counties, and thirty miles from Shrewsbury, as it is near ten to the borders of Shropshire. Though a paternal estate, it was never distinguished for any peculiar beauties till the time of the late owner. It was reserved for a person of his ingenuity both to discover and improve them; which he has done so effectually, that it is now considered as amongst the principal of those delightful scenes, which persons of taste, in the present age, are desirous to see. Far from violating its natural beauties, Mr. Shenstone's only study was to give them their full effect. And although the form in which things now appear be indeed the consequence of much thought and labour, yet the hand of art is no way visible either in the shape of the ground, the disposition of the trees, or (which are here so numerous and striking) the romantic falls of his cascades.

. . .

A View in Hagley Park the Seat of Lord Lyttelton.

Engraving of Hagley Park, 1776.

You now proceed a few paces down the valley to another bench, where you have this cascade in front, which, together with the internal arch and other appendages, make a pretty irregular picture. I must observe once for all, that a number of these extempore benches (two stumps with a transverse board) seem chiefly intended as hint to spectators, left in passing cursorily thro' the farm they might suffer any of that immense variety the place furnishes, to escape their notice. The stream attending us, with it's agreeable murmurs, as we descend along this pleasing valley, we come next to a small seat, where we have a sloping grove along the right, and on the left a striking vista to the steeple of Hales Owen, which is here seen in a new light. We now descend further down this shady and sequestered valley, accompanied on the right by the same brawling rivulet running over pebbles, till it empties it's self into a fine piece of water at the bottom.

. . .

Here entering a gate, you are led through a thicket of many sorts of willows, into a large root-house, inscribed to the Right Honourable the Earl of Stamford. It seems, that worthy peer was present at the first opening of the cascade which is the principal object from the root-house, where the eye is presented with a fairy vision, consisting on an irregular and romantic fall of water, very unusual, one hundred and fifty yards in continuity; and a very striking scene it affords.

A bridge composed of unhewn, unpolished wood.

Other cascades may possibly have the advantage of a greater descent and a larger torrent; but a more wild and romantic appearance of water, and at the same time strictly natural, is what I never saw in any place whatever. This scene, though comparatively small, is yet aggrandized with so much art, that we forget the quantity of water which flows through this close and overshaded valley; and are so much transported with the intricacy of scene, and the concealed height from whence it flows, that we, without reflection, add the idea of magnificence to that of beauty.

. . .

And now passing through a wicket, the path winds up the back part of a circular green hill, discovering little of the country till you enter a clump of stately firs upon the summit . . .. The scene is a very fine one, divided by the firs into several compartments, each answering to the octagonal seat in the center, to each of which is allotted a competent number of striking objects to make a complete picture. A long serpentine stream washes the foot of this hill, and is lost behind trees at one end, and a bridge thrown over at the other. Over this the eye is carried from very romantic home-scenes to very beautiful ones at a distance. It is impossible to give an idea of that immense variety, that fine configuration of parts, which engage our attention from this place. In one of the compartments you have a simple scene of a cottage, and a road winding behind a farmhouse, half covered with trees, upon the top of some wild sloping ground; and in another a view of the town, appearing from hence as upon the shelving banks of a large piece of water in the flat. Suffice it to say, that the hill and vale, plain and woodland, villages and single houses, blue distant mountains that skirt the horizon, and green hill romantically jumbled, that form the intermediate ground, make this spot more than commonly striking – nor is there to be seen an acre of level ground through the large extent to which the eye is carried.

. . .

Still winding up into the wood, we come to a slight seat opening through the trees to a bridge of five piers. Crossing a large piece of water at about half a mile's distance. The next seat looks down from a considerable height, along the side of a steep precipice, upon irregular and pleasing ground. And now we turn upon a sudden into a long strait-lined walk in the wood, arched over with tall trees, and terminating with a small rustic building. Though the walk, as I said, be strait-lined, yet the base rises and falls so agreeably, as leaves no room to censure it's formality. About the middle of this avenue, which runs the whole length of this hanging wood, we arrive unexpectedly at a lofty Gothic seat, whence we look down a slope, more considerable than that before-mentioned, through the wood on each side. This view is indeed a fine one; the eye first travelling down over well-variegated ground into the valley, where is a large piece of water, whose sloping banks give all the appearance of a noble river. The ground from hence rises gradually to the top of Clent Hill, at three or four miles distance, and the landskip is enriched with a view of Hales Owen, the late Lord Dudley's house, and a large wood of Lord Lyttelton's. It is impossible to give an adequate description of this view; the beauty of it depending upon the great variety of objects and beautiful shape of ground; and all at such a distance as to admit of being seen distinctly.

. . .

This seat is placed upon a steep bank on the edge of the valley; from which the eye is here drawn down into the flat below, by the light that glimmers in front, and by the sound of various cascades, by which the winding stream is agreeably broken. Opposite to this seat the ground rises again in an easy concave to a kind of dripping fountain, where a small rill trickles down a rude nich [sic] of rock-work, through fern, liverwort, and aquatic weeds. The green area in the middle, through which the stream winds, being as well shaped as can be imagined. After falling down these cascades, it winds under a bridge of one arch, and then empties itself into a small lake which catches it a little below. This terminates the scene upon the right; and after these objects have for some time amused the spectator, his eye rambles to the left, where one of the most beautiful cascades imaginable is seen, by way of incident, through a kind of vista or glade, falling down a precipice over-arched with trees, and strikes us with surprize. It is impossible to express the pleasure which one feels on this occasion; for though surprize alone is not excellence, it may serve to quicken the effect of what is beautiful. I believe, none ever beheld this grove, without a thorough sense of satisfaction; and were one to chuse any particular spot of this perfectly Arcadian farm, it should, perhaps, be this.'

– A Description of the Leasowes by R. Dodsley in *The Works in Verse and Prose of William Shenstone* (1777, 5th ed.)

On parterres:

'Parterres were common in ancient gardening, which were a sort of flower ground divided into various formal figures in numerous small partitions; but in modern gardening, Chinese parterres are more in taste, consisting of straight beds, borders and alleys in different directions; but parterres in the ancient style, consisted of beds and alleys, in long squares, circles, scrolls and flourishes, labyrinths, or mazes: and sometimes turned into coats of arms, &c. having all the compartments edged with dwarf box, and laying the alleys some with red sand or gravel, others with white, some with shells, &c. and the beds formed swelling; and planted with the choicer sorts of flowers and small shrubs.'

– *The Young Gardener's Best Companion* by S. Fullmer (1786)

 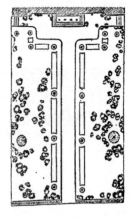

Examples of parterres.

Artistic combinations in flower gardening:

'For some years past the planting of flower beds in masses of one colour has been the prevailing fashion, not only in this country but also upon the continent. That the practice is very good one cannot be denied, as the violent contrasts of distinct or complementary colours has a very striking effect. The only drawback upon the system is a want of intricacy and variety, and hence some gardeners have adopted the mixed system, planting flowers of distinct and contrasting colours in concentric circles or distinct straight lines. In this new scheme it is questionable whether we are not exchanging the massive and decided for the "little prettinesses" of persons of small intelligence; and it is quite certain that beds so arranged, though they may be individually striking and interesting, cannot produce the grand effect of bold masses of properly contrasted and distinct colours. If we wish to detract from the size of a garden, these mixed beds are well calculated to assist in such a work; but, if boldness and distinctness of expression is wished for, then masses of distinct must be employed. Originating in this system of planting, is what may be called "ribbon grouping," in which a long narrow border of distinct colours are blended in imitation of the gaudy ribbons which sometimes garnish the shop fronts of silk-mercers, and such borders, when of sufficient length, have a very remarkable and striking effect. Thus, for example, a row of dark blue Branching Larkspur for the back, with *Calceolaria viscosissima* next, and then Scarlet Pelargorniums in the front, is said to look very fine, and no doubt, if the border has a margin of grass, a row of Mangle's Variegated or Silver Bedding Pelargonium, might be introduced in the front with advantage.

Again *Penstemon gentianoides coccinea* with Orange Calceolaria, Purple Senecio – the dark variety, – Dwarf Scarlet Pelargonium and *Lobelia gracilis,* or any of the dark blue trailing varieties, would afford an excellent combination.

Among hardy plants, the following may be planted in lines together: – *Delphinium Barlowii* or *chinense,* blue; *Lobelia splendens,* scarlet; Yellow Lupine; Crimson Antirrhinum; *Campanula carpatica,* purple, with, if the edging is grass, Variegated Alyssum in front.'

– Article from *Gardeners' Magazine of Botany: The Garden Companion and Florists' Guide*, February 1852

On the prevailing style of laying out grounds in England:

'The prevailing style of laying out grounds in England is what is emphatically called English gardening; to which epithet a vague general idea is attached, of grounds and plantations formed in flowing lines, in imitation of nature; as contradistinguished from ground formed into regular slopes and levels, or plantations in straight lines, or included in plots, bounded by lines always decidedly artificial. What is called the English, or natural, style of gardening, however may be divided into three kinds: the picturesque, the gardenesque*, and the rustic. By picturesque gardening is to be understood the production, in country residences, of that kind of scenery which, from its strongly marked features, is considered as particularly suitable for being represented by painting; while by the gardenesque style is to be understood the production of that kind of scenery which is best calculated to display the individual beauty of trees, shrubs and plants in a state of culture; the smoothness and greenness of lawns; and the smooth surfaces, curved directions, dryness, and firmness of gravel walks: in short, the gardenesque style is calculated for displaying the art of

---

* J. C. Loudon coined this term to describe a style of gardening which could not be mistaken for natural, in which plants are purposely cultivated and laid-out to create beauty and reveal the skill of the gardener.

the gardener; while the picturesque style has a constant reference to what would look well in a picture; and the rustic style to what is commonly found accompanying the rudest description of labourer' cottages in the country. The object of this last-mentioned style, or rather manner, is also to produce such fac-simile imitations of common nature, as to deceive the spectator into an idea that they are real or fortuitous.'

– The Suburban Gardener and Villa Companion
by J. C. Loudon (1838)

A letter on Hagley:

Originally a medieval deer park, Hagley Park in Worcestershire became a prime example of English land-scape gardening from 1747, when George Lyttelton began to develop the grounds in memory of his wife. That Lyttelton was not remodelling an existing formal garden played to the strengths of this landscape, which was already blessed with naturally occurring hills, valleys and watercourses to which he added romantic ruins, seats and urns. Unfortunately in the nineteenth century the park fell into disrepair, however

Ruins and antiquities.

since 2013 efforts have been made to restore it to its eighteenth century glory.

'The weather becoming so exceedingly fine, and the whole face of the country appearing so irresistibly inviting, determined me in my excursion; – my heart was set upon the pleasing tour; and as I pressed towards the lovely bowers of Hagley, my feelings declared me perfectly happy – I did not arrive there till the dusk of the evening; and in the sweetest morning that ever ushered in the meridian of spring, walked up an easy winding avenue of limes, and elms, among a thousand mellow throated birds, till the house burst upon me in all its glory.

I paused. —

I saw grandeur supported by simplicity – I saw a proof in this modern pile, that true elegance spurns the aid of superfluous ornament.'

– Letters on the Beauties of Hagley, Envil,
and the Leasowes by Joseph Heely (1777)

On the skill of good gardeners:

'Where twining serpentine walks, digging holes and crooked ditches for earth to raise mole-hills, scattering shrubs, and ringing never-ceasing changes on lawns, groves and thickets, is called Gardening; artists will have few opportunities of displaying their talents; it matters little there who are the Gardeners; a cabbage planter may rival a Claude, and a clown out-twine a Poussin: the meanest may do the little there is to be done, and the best could reach no farther. But wherever a better style is adopted, and Gardens are to be natural, without resemblance to vulgar Nature, new without affectation, and extraordinary without extravagance; where the spectator is to be amused, where his attention is constantly to be kept up, his curiosity excited, and his mind agitated by a great variety of opposite passions, there parts will be necessary;

and Gardeners must be men of genius, of experience and judgement; quick in perception, rich in expedients, fertile in imagination, and thoroughly versed in all the affections of the human mind.'

– A Dissertation on Oriental Gardening
by Sir William Chambers (1772)

On gardening jobs for February:

'February. Pisces.

In this Month prune Vines and Wall-Fruit-Trees before the Buds swell; but for the Nectarines and other Choice Fruit, you may omit it until the next Month; in nailing the Branches, do not overstrain them, that hindring the Motion of the Sap; and in a judicial Pruning lies the Master-piece of Gardening. If the Frost hath killed your Cabbage plants set in *September*, sow seeds now in a hot Bed, made thus: Dig a Trench according to Discretion, about two Foot deep, in the warmest Place of your Garden, free from the chilling Blasts of the North and the East Winds; tread it full of Horse-litter with the Dung, and cover it with rich Earth, half a Foot thick; the Earth must be skreened or sifted pretty fine, and cover it with Straw or Mats, in cold Nights only: In such

Beds may be sown the Seed of Cucumbers, Musk Melons, or Purslain. The Grafts of former Years grafting may now be removed. Sow Pease and set Beans about a Foot distant. Also now plant the Slips of Gooseberries and Currants. Moss your Fruit-trees, and drain your Orchard and Garden of wet proceeding from melted Snow or Rain, and settled at the Roots of Trees, &c.'

— The Gentleman's, Traveller's, Husbandman's and
Gardener's Pocket Companion (1751)

On landscape (or landskip):

'I use the word landskip and prospect, the former as expressive of homes scenes, the latter of dist'nt images. Prospects should take in the blue distant hills; but never so remotely, that they be not distinguishable from clouds. Yet this mere extent, is what the vulgar value.

Landskip should contain variety enough to form a picture upon canvas; and this is no bad test, as I think the landskip-painter is the gardener's best designer. The eye requires a sort of balance here; but not so as to encroach upon probable nature. A wood, or a hill, may balance a house or obelisk; for exactness would be displeasing. We form our

Trees can improve the outlines of buildings.

notions from what we have seen; and though, could we comprehend the universe, we might perhaps find it uniformly
regular; yet the portions that we see of it, habituate our fancy
to the contrary.'

– The Works in Verse and Prose of
William Shenstone (1777, 5th ed.)

On the artificial rock work at Stowe:

'THEN, turning on the Left-hand, you come to an arti-
ficial Piece of Ruins, which is mostly hid by a Clump of
Ever-greens: It is adorned with the Statues of FAUNS,
SATYRS, and River-Gods; a beautiful Cascade of three
Sheets of Water, which will run at any time Nine Hours,

falls from the Bason, through Arches, into a large Lake of ten Acres, where floats a Model of a Man of War with all her Rigging: Just by, is a cold Bath. This Ruin is a great beauty to the Lake; there is something so delightful and pleasing to the Imagination in such Objects, that they are a great Addition to every landscape; and yet, perhaps, it would be hard to assign a Reason, why we are more taken with Prospects of this ruinous Kind, than with Views of Plenty and Prosperity in their greatest Perfection; Such Regularity and Exactness excites no manner of Pleasure in the Imagination, unless they are made use of to contrast with something of an opposite Kind. The Fancy is struck by Nature alone; and, is Art does any thing more improve her, we think she grows impertinent; and wish she had left off a little sooner. Thus, a regular Building, perhaps, gives us a very little Pleasure; and yet we find Rocks, beautifully set off in Clara-obscura, and garnished with flourishing Bushes, Ivy, and dead Branches, may afford us a great deal; and a ragged Ruin, with Venerable old Oaks and Pines nodding over it, may perhaps please the Fancy yet more than either of the other two Objects.'

– *The Beauties of Stow* by George Bickham (1753)

On women and gardening:

'There is scarcely such a thing to be found as a lady who is not fond of flowers; but it is not saying too much, to affirm that there are very few ladies indeed who are competent to lay out a flower-garden; though the skill required to do so is within the capacity of every woman who can cut out, and put together, the different parts of a female dress: and, supposing a female to have grown up without the slightest knowledge of the art of cutting out a gown, or of tracing out a flower garden, it would certainly be much easier for her to acquire the latter art than the former. The result, in both cases, might be obtained almost without instruction, provided the party desiring to form the dress, or the flower-garden, had a clear idea of what was wanted. But, while every female understands this in regards to dress, and, consequently, can succeed in making gowns when she is obliged to make the attempt, very few have any distinct idea of what a flower-garden ought to be; and, hence, we seldom or never see them produce a satisfactory design for one, without the aid of a professional man.'

– *The Suburban Gardener and Villa Companion*
by J. C. Loudon (1838)

The beautiful in ground-surface:

'Artists and men of taste have agreed that all forms of acknowledged beauty are composed of *curved lines*. The principle applies as well to the surface of the earth as to other objects. The most beautiful shape in ground is that where one undulation melts gradually and invisibly into another. Everyone who has observed scenery where the fore-ground has been remarkable for beauty, must have been struck by the prevalence of curved lines; and every landscape gardener well knows that no grass surface is so captivating to one eye as one where these gentle swells and undulations rise and melt away gradually into one another . . ..

The surface of the ground is rarely *ugly* in a state of nature, because all nature leans to the beautiful; and the ceaseless action of the elements goes continually to soften and wear away the harshness and violence of surface. What cannot be softened is hidden and rounded by means of foliage, trees, and shrubs, and creeping Vines, and so the tendency to curve is always greater and greater. But man often forms ugly surfaces of ground by breaking up all natural curves without recognizing their expression, by distributing lumps of earth here and there, by grading levels in the midst of undulations, and raising mounds on perfectly smooth surfaces; in short, by regarding only the little he wishes to do in his folly, and not studying the larger part that Nature has already done in her wisdom.'

– 'The Beautiful in Ground-Surface' by A. J. Downing.
Article from *Gardeners' Magazine of Botany: The Garden Companion and Florists' Guide*, June 1852

Repton on contrasts:

'The next contrast I shall mention is that of Light and dark not in shadow and shade, but of a variety in colouring observable in Nature, and well worth cultivating in the art of Gardening, although difficult to represent in painting. Of this I shall enumerate several kinds.

First, The difference of a leaf with the light *shining full upon it*, which renders it an opake object, and the same leaf seen transparent by the light *shining through it*.

Secondly, The Contrast produced amidst the more gaudy Colouring by the sort of repose that the eye derives, sometimes from white flowers, as of the jasmine, the passion-flower, and other plants, whose leaves are dark and glossy: sometimes the same repose is produced by a mass of light foliage, at a little distance appearing without shape or colour, as in a bed of mignonette.

Thirdly, The Contrast in Texture; some plants and flowers appearing as if composed of silk, others of cloth or velvet; some as smooth as satin, others harsh, rough, and prickly.

Fourthly, The contrast of Size; some like the aloe, the horse-chesnut, or the tulip-tree, bearing their blossom above the reach of man; and others, like the diminutive dwarf Burgundy rose, and the gigantic Viola tricolor; which may be used as an example of contrasts in colour and in relative dimensions.'

— Fragments on the Theory and Practice of Landscape Gardening
by Humphry Repton (1816)

On the situation of a kitchen garden:

'If situated somewhat on an early ascent, to face the morning and mid-day sun, guarded well behind with walls or trees, or something like it, to keep off cold sharp winds in Spring; will be a spot desirable to nourish tender crops . . ..

To guess the soil, observe if trees or plants decay near or on the spot: if so, then this avoid, and fix on that, if to be had convenient, where healthy grass or plants grow kind,

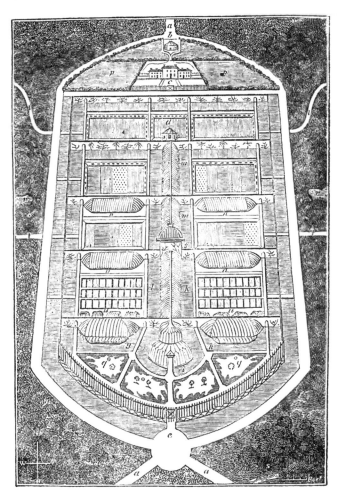

A kitchen garden.

and trees that's large do flourish. To try the soil, let holes
be dug to twenty inches deep, in several different parts, to
find a hazely loam, or earth that is black and fertile. And

when the spot is fixt upon, trench it eighteen inches deep, if that it will but bear it; if not, as deep or shallow as it will. Gravel, clay, and swamps, and couchy cattail land, should always be avoided.'

— The Beauties of Flora Display'd by N. Swinden (1778)

On the placing of statues:

'These Figures represent all the several Deities, and illustrious Persons of Antiquity, which should be placed properly in Gardens.

The River Gods, as *Naiades*, *Rivers*, and *Tritons*, should be placed in the Middle of Fountains or Basons.

The Gods of the Woods, as *Sylvans*, *Fauns*, and *Dryads*, in the Groves; *Sacrifices*, *Bacchanals*, and Childrens Sports are likewise presented in *Bas Relievo* upon the Vases and Pedestals, which may be adorn'd with Festoons, Foliage, Mouldings, and other Ornaments.'

— The Gardeners Dictionary by Philip Miller (1737)

Brown on laying out a garden:

Capability Brown never wrote publically about his ideas on landscape gardening, so we are left with very little in the way of documentary evidence revealing the thinking behind his designs. However, a letter has survived which sheds a little light on Brown's process – in 1775 the Rev. Thomas Dyer wrote to Brown asking for advice on behalf of a French friend on how to lay out a garden in the English style. Brown replied on 2 June 1775:

'I have made a Plan according to your desire, as well as I could, from the survey and descriptions you sent me, which I wish may be of use to the owner. In France they do not exactly comprehend our ideas on Gardening and Place-making which when rightly understood will supply all the elegance and all the comforts which Mankind wants in the Country and (I will add) if right, be exactly fit for the owner, the Poet and the Painter. To produce these effects there wants a good plan, good execution, a perfect knowledge of the country and the objects in it, whether natural or artificial, and infinite delicacy in the planting etc., so much Beauty depending on the size of the trees and the colour of their leaves to produce the effect of light and shade so very essential to the perfecting a good plan: as also the hideing [sic] what is disagreeable and shewing what is beautifull, getting shade from the large trees and sweets from the smaller sorts of shrubs etc. I hope they will in time find out in France that Placemaking, and a good English garden, depend intirely upon Principle and have very little to do with Fashion; for it is a word that in my opinion disgraces Science wherever it is found.'

– *Capability Brown* by Dorothy Stroud
(Faber & Faber, London, 1975)

On the formation of the flower garden:

'Shelter is equally requisite for the flower as for the kitchen garden, and, where naturally wanting, is to be produced by the same means, viz. planting. The plantation on the side next the garden, should begin with the lowest shrubs, and rise in gradation to the trees, which, unless on the north, or very exposed points, should not be of the tallest kinds. A few elegant shrubs, and one or two trees may be scattered through the scene, either in the dug compartments or in the turf-glades, for the purposes of shelter and shade as well as ornament; but in general, much of either of the two former qualities are highly injurious both to the culture of flowers, and the thick closeness of turf; besides rendering the garden unfit to be resorted to in the winter and spring seasons.

Sometimes an evergreen-hedge will produce all the shelter requisite, as in small gardens composed of earth and gravel only; but where the scene is large, and composed of dug compartments, placed on lawn, the whole may be surrounded by an irregular border of flowers, shrubbery, and trees.

. . .

Most of the hardy herbaceous flowers, and the deciduous and evergreen ornamental shrubs, will succeed in a soil of common good qualities, moderately light and mellow. Negatively, the ground should not be excessively strong and clayey; and mere gravel is very intractable.'

– An Encyclopaedia of Gardening; Comprising the Theory and Practice of Horticulture, Floriculture, Arboriculture, and Landscape-Gardening by J. C. Loudon (1822)

On the colour of trees:

'The different tints of greens may seem at first sight to be rather minute varieties than characteristic distinctions; but upon experience it will be found, that from small beginnings they lead to material consequences; that they are more important on the broad expanse, than along the narrow outline of a wood; and that by their union, or their contrast, they produce effects not to be disregarded in scenes of extent and of grandeur.

A hanging wood in autumn is enriched with colours, whose beauty cheers the approaches of inclement season they forebode: but when the trees first droop, while the verdure as yet only begins to fade, they are no more than stronger tints of those colours with which the greens in their vigour are shaded; and which now are succeeded by a paler white, a brighter yellow, or a darker brown. The effects are not different; they are only more faintly impressed at

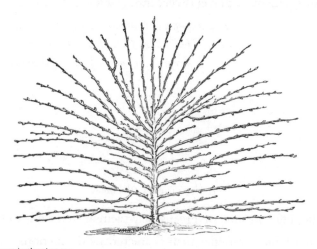

Fan-trained apricot tree.

one time than another; but when they are strongest, they are most observable. The fall of the leaf, therefore, is the time to learn the species, the order, and the proportion of tints, which blended, will form *beautiful masses*; and, on the other hand, to distinguish those which are *incompatible* near together.

. . .

In massing these tints, an attention must be constantly kept up to their forms, that they do not lie in large stripes one beyond another; but that either they be quite intermingled, or, which is generally more pleasing, that considerable pieces of different tints, each a beautiful figure, be, in different proportions, placed near together. Exactness in their shapes must not be attempted, for it cannot be preserved; but if the great outlines be well drawn, little variations, afterwards occasioned by the growth of the plants, will not spoil them.'

– *Observations on Modern Gardening*
by Thomas Whately (1770)

In praise of Brown:

Lord Viscount Irwin, the owner of Temple Newsam House, employed Capability Brown to redesign the gardens in the 1760s. In 1767 a long, anonymous poem appeared, dedicated to Lord Irwin and praising Brown's achievements at Temple Newsam as well as several of his other works:

'And all around romantic scenes display.
Delighted still along the Park we rove,
Vary'd with Hill and Dale, with Wood and Grove:
O'er velvet Lawns what noble Prospects rise,
Fair as the Scenes, that Reuben's hand supplies!

But when the Lake shall these sweet Grounds adorn,
And bright expanding like the eye of Morn,
Reflect whate'er above its surface rise,
The Hills, the Rocks, the Woods, and varying Skies,
Then will the wild and beautiful combine,

And Taste and Beauty grace your whole Design.
But your great Artist, like the source of light,
Gilds every Scene with beauty and delight;
At Blenheim, Croome, and Caversham we trace
Salvator's Wildness, Claud's enlivening grace,

Cascades and Lakes as fine as Risdale drew,
While Nature's vary'd in each charming view.
To paint his works wou'd Pousin's Powers require,
Milton's sublimity, and Dryden's sire:
For both the Sister Arts in him combin'd,

Enrich the great ideas of his mind;
And these still brighten all his vast designs,
For here the Painter, there the Poet shines!
With just contempt he spurns all former rules,
And shows true Taste is not confin'd to schools.

He barren tracts with every charm illumes,
At his command a new Creation blooms;
Born to grace Nature, and her works complete,
With all that's beautiful, sublime and great!
For him each Muse enwreathes the Laurel Crown,
And consecrates to Fame immortal Brown.'

> – Extract from *The Rise and Progress of the Present Taste
> in Planting Parks, Pleasure Grounds, Gardens, Etc.*,
> anonymous (1767)

Price on Brown:

Price was very much preoccupied with the debate on the nature of beauty and the appreciation of natural scenes which might inspire the great landscape painters. Consequentially, he was very dismissive of the designs of Capability Brown, finding them too conventional.

'No possessor of high reputation, seems for some time to have appeared after [William] Kent, till. At length, that the system might be carried to its *ne plus ultra* (no very distant point) arose the famous Mr. Brown; who has so fixed and determined the forms and lines of clumps, belts, and serpentine canals, and has been so steadily imitated by his followers, that had the improvers been incorporated, their common seal, with a clump, a belt, and a piece of made water, would have fully expressed the whole of their science, and have served for a model as well as a seal.

Alisander, or alexanders.

It is very unfortunate, that this great legislator of our national taste, whose laws still remain in force, should not have received from nature, or have acquired by education, more enlarged ideas. Claude Lorraine was bred a pastry-cook, but in every thing that regards his art as a painter, he had an elevated and comprehensive mind;

nor in any part of his works can we trace the meanness of his original occupation. Mr. Brown was bred a gardener, and having nothing of the mind, or the eye of a painter, he formed his style (or rather his plan) upon the model of parterre; and transferred its minute beauties, its little clumps, knots, and patches of flowers, the oval belt that surrounds it, and all its twists and crincum crancums, to the great scale of nature.'

– *An Essay on the Picturesque* by Uvedale Price, 1796

On gardening jobs for March:

'March. Aries, or the Ram.

Dung your Orchard and plant Trees that remain unset; cover the Roots of Trees that have continued bare since *Autumn*. Sow Carrots, Parsnips, Parsley-seed and Turnips for Seed. Set Onions and Leeks, and more Beans and Pease. Now you may take off the Litter from your Asparagus-Bed, and, after a little digging or stirring it, sift some good Earth upon it: But if you make a new Bed, make it as directed in the last Month. Set short-stalked Cabbage-plants near a Yard asunder on the Edges of your Carrot Ground. This

whole Month you may graft, cut off the Tops of your bud-
ded Stalks, and prune Grafts of the last Year.'

– *The Gentleman's, Traveller's, Husbandman's and
Gardener's Pocket Companion* (1751)

*Whately on picturesque scenes, differences
for painters and gardeners:*

'Painting, with all its powers, is still more unequal to some
subjects, and can give only a *faint, if any, representation of them*;
but a gardener is not therefore to reject them; he is not
debarred from a view down the sides of a hill, or a prospect where the horizon is lower than the station, because
he never saw them in a picture. Even when painting exactly
imitates the appearances of nature, it is often weak in conveying the ideas which they excite, and on which much of
their effect depends. This however is not always a disadvan-
tage; the appearance may be more pleasing than the idea
which accompanies it: and the omission of the one may be
an improvement of the other; many beautiful tints denote
disagreeable circumstances; the hue of a barren heath is
often finely diversified; a piece of bare ground is sometimes

overspread with a number of delicate shades; and yet we prefer a more uniform verdure to all their variety. In a picture, the several tints which occur in nature may be blended, and retain only their beauty, without suggesting the poverty of the soil which occasions them; but in reality, the cause is more powerful than the effect; we are less pleased with the sight, than we are hurt by the reflection; and a most agreeable mixture of colours may present no other idea than of dreariness and sterility.

. . .

Many more instances might be alleged to prove, that the subjects for a painter and gardener are not always the same; some which are agreeable in the reality, lose their effect in the imitation; and others, at the best, have less merit in a scene than in a picture. The term picturesque is therefore applicable only to such objects in nature, as, after allowing for the differences between the arts of painting and of gardening, are fit to be formed into groups, or to enter into a composition, where the several parts have a relationship to each other; and in opposition to those which may be spread abroad in detail, and have no merit but as individuals.'

– *Observations on Modern Gardening*
by Thomas Whately (1770)

Repton on the distinction between painting and gardening:

'The greatest objection to Landscape Gardening seems to arise from not making the proper distinction between *Painting* and *Gardening*. The difference betwixt a scene in nature, and a picture on canvas, arises from the following considerations.

First, The spot from whence the view is taken is in a fixed state to the painter; but the gardener surveys his scenery while in motion; and from different windows in the same front he sees objects in different situations; therefore, to give an accurate portrait of the gardener's improvement, would require pictures from each separate window, and even a different drawing at the most trifling change of situation, either in the approach, the walks, or the drives about the place.

Secondly, The quantity of view, or *field of vision* in nature, is much greater than any picture will admit.

Thirdly, The view from an eminence down a steep hill is not to be represented in painting, although it is often one of the most pleasing circumstances of natural landscape.

Fourthly, The light which the painter may bring from any point on the compass must, in real scenery, depend on the time of day. It must also be remembered that the light of a picture can only be made strong by contrast of shade; while in nature every object may be strongly illuminated, without destroying the composition, or disturbing the keeping. And

Lastly, The foreground, which by framing the view, is absolutely necessary to the picture, is often totally deficient, or seldom such as a painter chooses to represent; since the neat gravel-walk, or close mown lawn, would ill supply the place in painting, of a rotten tree, a bunch of docks, or a broken road, passing under a steep bank, covered with briers, nettles, and ragged thorns.'

– An Enquiry into the Changes of taste in Landscape Gardening
by H. Repton (1806)

Price on what makes a good landscape:

'It seems to me, that the neglect, which prevails in the works of modern improvers, of all that is picturesque, is owing to their exclusive attention to high polish and flowing lines, the charms of which they are so engaged in contemplating, as to make them overlook two of the most fruitful sources of human pleasure; the first, that great and universal source of pleasure, variety, whose power in independent of beauty, but without which even beauty itself soon ceases to please; the other, intricacy, a quality which, though distinct from variety, is so connected and blended with it, that the one can hardly exist without the other.

According to the idea I have formed of it, intricacy in landscape might be defined, *that disposition of objects which, by a partial and uncertain concealment, excites and nourishes curiosity.* Variety can hardly require a definition, though, from the practice of many layers-out of ground, one might suppose it did. Upon the whole, it appears to me, that as intricacy in the disposition, and variety in the forms, the tints, and lights and shadows of objects, are the great characteristics of picturesque scenery; so monotony and baldness are the greatest defects of improved places.'

– *An Essay on the Picturesque* by Uvedale Price, 1796

Knight in reply to Price on the picturesque:

In a postscript to his poem *The Landscape*, Richard Payne Knight addressed his friend and neighbour, Uvedale Price in light of his work on the picturesque:

'. . . If it was reserved for him [Price] to lay down better precepts; if he is the first who has properly invoked the

rural Graces *solutis zonis*, why should poor
BROWN, who made way for them by the
destruction of the formal and the ugly,
meet with such harsh, such very severe
criticism? Would it not be more just, as
well as candid, to detect his errors, but
at the same time give him his due share of
praise? The whole list of crimes commit-
ted by this great culprit in the regions of

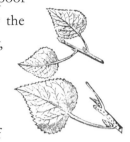

Poplar-leaved birch (top)
and Hudson's birch (bottom).

taste, and for which he is now impeached at the bar of the
public, may be comprised in one article, viz. that he made
the Beautiful his sole aim, without sufficiently attending to
the Picturesque.

. . .

It is the *Beautiful*, which is more within the reach of the
Improver. This is surely to be found in the undulating play
of smooth verdure, in the contrast of different trees happily
disposed, and the endless variety of foliage and flowers of
humbler growth. All these circumstances are charming in
reality, though they may not furnish good subjects for the
pencil. The fastidious eye, which turns from such a scene
with disgust, because there is no temptation to take out the
sketch-book is, I think, not much to be envied.'

– *A Word to Uvedale Price, Esq.*
by R. P. Knight, Esq. (1794)

Gilpin on Blenheim:

Blenheim Palace in Oxfordshire, designed by architect Sir John Vanbrugh, was built between 1705 and 1733. The palace included extensive parkland, which between 1764 and 1774 was substantially remodelled by Capability Brown at the apex of his career.

'This immense pile stands in the middle of an extensive park. The situation is, in general, flat. A lawn, proportioned to the house, spreads in front; and, at the distance of about half a mile, meets an abrupt valley, which winds across the park. The sides of this valley are shagged with well-grown wood. At the bottom ran once a penurious stream; over which, directly opposite the castle, is thrown a magnificent bridge, consisting of a single arch; intended chiefly to make easy communication between two sides of the valley.

About half a mile beyond this arch is reared a triumphal column; which, tho much criticized, I own, gives me no offence; but rather seems to carry on the idea of grandeur. The top is crowned with the statue of the duke of Marlborough; and the pedestal is inscribed – not indeed with the terseness of a Roman altar – but with the less classical, tho more honourable detail of an act of parliament;

granting the manor of Woodstock to the duke for his eminent services.

All this scenery before the castle, is now new-modelled
by the late ingenious Mr. Brown, who has given a specimen
of his art, in a nobler style, then he has commonly displayed.
His works are generally pleasing; but here they are great.

About a mile below the house, he has thrown across the
valley, a massy head; which forms the rivulet into a noble
lake, divided by the bridge, (which now appears properly
with all the grandeur of accompaniments) into two very
extensive pieces of water. Brown himself used to say, "that
the Thames would never forgive him, what he had done
at Blenheim." And every spectator must allow, that. On
entering the great gate from Woodstock, the whole of this
scenery, (the castle, the lawn, the woods, and the lake) seen
together, makes one of the grandest bursts, which art perhaps ever displayed.

The scenery *below* the bridge is the most beautiful part.
The water here takes the form of a bay, running up into a
wooded country; and several light skiffs at anchor, impress
the idea. The bay appears totally land-locked, and the ground
falls easily into it in every part.

Behind the house, the improved grounds consist, (in
Mr. Brown's usual style,) of a *belt*, as it is called, incircling
a portion of the park. In this part grandeur gives way to
beauty; except where the walk traverses the side of the bay.

Here the great idea is still extended; and the banks of the Wye scarce exhibit more romantic scenes, than are here displayed in the level plains of Oxfordshire. The walk carried us along the side of one woody precipice, severed from another, by an expanse of water, which no English river could furnish.

Of this situation every advantage is taken, which could add variety to grandeur. In one part, the opposite woody shore is seen alone, spreading before the eye in a vast profusion of woody scenery. In another part it appears accompanied with the lake: and sometimes it is only received in catches, through the woods of the fore-ground, which are generally composed of lofty oak.

In the midst of these great ideas, the scene was not improved by several little patches of flowers, and flowering shrubs, artificially disposed, and introduced; which shewed the hand of art to have been straying, where the imagination would wish to be ingrossed by the grand exhibition of simplicity, and nature.'

– *Observations on the Mountains and Lakes of Cumberland and Westmoreland* by William Gilpin (1786)

On small gardens:

'But in small gardens, where there is not proper scope for various rural imitation; either have only a small lawn at the entrance from the house, bounded by shrubbery work, in clumps, &c. with a serpentine gravel walk through the shrubbery or along the sides; or sometimes having no lawn, extend a grand walk immediately from the front door through the middle of the garden, with a spacious border on each side for flowers and shrubs, and a walk also continued across and round the garden, verged likewise with handsome flower borders; or in very small grounds, have only a walk either

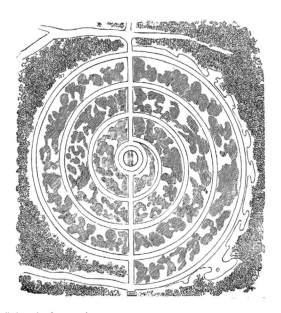

Gravel walk through a flower garden.

along the middle, or all round, furnished on each side with a handsome broad border for flowering plants.'

— *The Young Gardener's Best Companion* by S. Fullmer (1786)

ℛepton on naming landscape gardening:

'To improve the scenery of a country, and to display its native beauties with advantage, is an art which originated in England, and has therefore been called *English Gardening*; yet, as this expression is not sufficiently appropriate, especially since Gardening, in its more confined sense of *Horticulture*, has been likewise brought to the greatest perfection in this country, I have adopted the term LANDSCAPE GARDENING, because the art can only be advanced and perfected by the united powers of the *landscape painter* and the *practical gardener*. The former must conceive a plan which the latter may be able to execute; for though a painter may represent a beautiful landscape on his canvas, and even surpass nature by the combination of her choicest materials; yet the luxuriant imagination of the *painter* must be subjected to the *gardener*'s practical knowledge in planting, digging, and moving earth; that the simplest and readiest means of accomplishing each design may be suggested; since it is not

by vast labour, or great expence, that nature is generally to
be improved; on the contrary.'

— An Enquiry into the Changes of taste in Landscape Gardening
by H. Repton (1806)

Walpole on the natural garden:

'Thus dealing in none but the colours of nature, and catch-
ing its most favourable features, men saw a new creation
opening before their eyes. The living landscape was chas-
tened or polished, not transformed. Freedom was given
to the forms of trees; they extended their branches unre-
stricted, and where any eminent oak, or master beech had
escaped maiming and survived the forest, bush and bramble
was removed, and all its honours were restored to distinguish
and shade the plain. Where the united plumage of an ancient
wood extended wide its undulating canopy, and stood venerable in its darkness, Kent thinned the foremost ranks, and
left so many detached and scattered trees, as softened the
approach of gloom and blended a chequered light with the
thus lengthened shadows of the remaining columns.'

— The History of the Modern Taste in Gardening
by Horace Walpole (1780)

On a beautiful rural garden:

'The several parts of a beautiful Rural garden, are *Walks, Slopes, Borders, Open Plains, Plain Parterres, Avenues, Groves, Wildernesses, Labyrinths, Fruit-Gardens, Flower-Gardens, Vineyards, Hop-Gardens, Nurseries, Coppiced Quarters, Green Openings,* like Meadows: Small inclosures of *Corn, cones of Ever-Greens,* of *Flowering Shrubs,* of *Fruit-Trees,* of *Forest-Trees,* and mix'd together: *Mounts, Terraces,* Winding *Valleys, Dales, Purling Streams, Basons, Canals, Fountains, Cascades, Grotto's, Rocks, Ruins, Serpentine Meanders, Rude Coppies* [sic], *Hay-Stacks, Wood-Piles, Rabbit* and *Hare-Warrens, Cold Baths, Aviaries, Cabinets, Statues, Obelisks, Manazeries, Pheasant* and

A labyrinth in a pleasure ground.

Partridge-Grounds, Orangeries, Melon-Grounds, Kitchen-Gardens, Physick or *Herb-Garden, Orchard, Bowling-Green, Dials, Precipices, Amphitheatres, &c.'*

– *New Principles of Gardening* by Batty Langley (1728)

On planting the flower garden:

'The manner of planting the herbaceous plants and shrubs in a flower-garden depends jointly on the style and extent of the scene. With a view to planting, they may be divided into three classes, which classes are independently altogether of the style in which they are laid out. The first class is *the general or mingled flower-garden*, in which is displayed a mixture of flowers with or without flowering-shrubs according to its size. The object in this class is to mix the plants, as that every part of the garden may present a gay assemblage of flowers of different colors during the whole season. The second class is *the select flower-garden*, in which the object is limited to the cultivation of particular kinds of plants; as, florists' flowers, American plants, annuals, bulbs, &c. Sometimes two or more classes are included in one garden, as bulbs and annuals; but, in general, the best effect is produced by limiting the object to one class only. The third class is *the changeable flower-garden*, in which all the plants are kept in pots, and reared in a flower-nursery or reserve-ground. As soon as they begin to flower, they are plunged in the borders of the flower-garden, and, whenever they show symptoms of decay, removed, to be replaced by others from the same source. This is obviously the most complete mode of any for a display of flowers, as the beauties of both the general and particular gardens may be combined without presenting blanks, or losing the fine effect of assemblages of varieties of the same species; as of hyacinth, pink, dahlia, chrysanthemum, &c. The fourth class is *the botanic flower-garden*, in which the plants are arranged with reference to botanical study, or at least not in any way that has for its main object a rich display of blossoms.'

– An Encyclopaedia of Gardening; Comprising the Theory and Practice of Horticulture, Floriculture, Arboriculture, and Landscape-Gardening by J. C. Loudon (1822)

A circular clump or cone of flowers, arranged by height.

On the situation of a pleasure garden:

'This must necessarily vary, from the advantages or incon-
veniences natural to itself; from the country it is fixt in and
the disposal of it to the peculiar genius of the owner. But if
situated on an easy ascent, to face the morning and mid-day
sun, opened to an extensive view of various pleasing objects,
well diversified by hills, vales, woods, fruitful fields of corn;
or rich verdant pastures, edged with a noble river, gliding
and meandering through the different scenes, till lost and hid
in part, by some few trees, large and flourishing; perhaps in
quicksets, bounding a road to some old castle, great metropolis, or sea-port town; or changed by a scene of mountains,
fine built ships, full sailing on the seas, a wide space of desert
land between the view, or fertile plains, o'er-spread with
flocks and herds, to shew the goodness of the Great Creator.

A spot commanding objects somewhat similar to those
above, will be a situation most desirable to correspond with
my present intentions, where the eye, being wearied from a
view of distant objects, is now delighted with those at home;
quick glancing o'er the lawn's smooth, verdant surface, is
invited to tufts and clumps of Flora's great and gay varieties,
of painted objects, and odoriferous sweets; from whence the

favourable shrubs, placed round in serpentine, on either side, afford a shade for contemplation.'

– *The Beauties of Flora Display'd* by N. Swinden (1778)

$\mathcal{O}$n statues:

'STATUES and VASES contribute very much to the Embellishment and Magnificence of a Garden, and extremely advance the natural Beauties of it.

They are made of several Forms and different Materials; the richest are those of Cast Brass, Lead gilt, and Marble; the ordinary Sort are of common Stone or *Stucco*.

Among Figures are distinguish'd Groups, which consist at least of two Figures together in the same Block; Figures insulate or detch'd, that is, those that you can go quite round; and Figures that are set in Niches, which are furnish'd on the fore Part only.

There are likewise Busts, Termes, half-length Figures, Figures half as big as the life, and those bigger than the Life that are call'd Colossal, either on regular pedestals, or such as are more slender, tapering, and hollow'd, not to mention the Figures which sometimes adorn Cascades.'

– *The Gardeners Dictionary* by Philip Miller (1737)

On gardening jobs for April:

'April. Taurus, or the Bull.

In this Month you may sow Scurvy-grass*, Carnations, Radishes, Majoram, Thyme, Winter-Savoury, Purslain, Marygolds, Hyssop and Lettuce; you may likewise set Slips of Rosemary, Lavender, Thyme, Artichokes, &c. Remove your tender Shrubs, and slip them after gentle Showers; and also set French Beans.'

— *The Gentleman's, Traveller's, Husbandman's and Gardener's Pocket Companion* (1751)

Observations on water as regards ornamental scenery:

'Of the many ornaments employed to embellish landscape scenery, and of those which relate more especially to landscape gardening, water contributes in an eminent degree to add the beautiful, the picturesque, or the grand. It is on

---

* Plants of the *Cochlearia* species, which are high in vitamin C and thus were so-called because they were eaten by sailors returning from long sea voyages.

the due appropriation of the forms of water, that a very important branch of the duties of the landscape gardener depend . . ..

If proofs were required of the value of water in landscape scenery, it would be necessary only to refer to those lovely scenes of nature, where the smooth unrippled lake, reflecting all the harmonious tints surrounding it, adds beauty to the scenery; where the winding river, with its variously formed banks, enlivens the meadow and the valley – where the purling stream of rivulet trickling down its pebbly bed, and breaking the silence, adds solemnity to the wood, – or where the bold impetuous cataract, dashing its waters over huge masses of rock, enriches so much the grandeur of the scene, already stupendous, that it becomes almost terrific. Such scenes as these must be viewed with admiration by all possessed of taste, and must be desirable on the domain of every lover of the beautiful and the picturesque.

A lake is very appropriate and ornamental in some situations, but as it requires extent in width and length, a unity of character is necessary in the surrounding scenery, that it may not appear to occupy too much space, nor be unappropriated; its boundaries should be much diversified in form, no distinguishable character of outline should be observable; the little intricacies occasioned by outlets and projections will be interesting, and productive of a pleasing effect, which in some places would wear the appearance of continuing where perhaps no water existed, thus providing a justifiable deception . . ..

In the disposal or formation of ornamental water, the banks must be a particular feature in producing the character required; on these much depend as to the general effect of the subject; and much judgment is essential to their well and appropriate disposal. To some situations the gentle curved line would be best adapted; to others a partial flat on one side, with perhaps a decided irregularity on the other; and sometimes the precipitous and towering bank, in parts over-hanging, would give contrast and effect.'

– 'Observations on water as regards Ornamental Scenery' by Richard Morris, surveyor and landscape gardener. Article from *The Gardener's Magazine* by J. C. Loudon, May 1827

On the design of a rural garden:

'The Design of a *rural Garden*, after the new manner, where the front of the House opens upon a fine *large plain Parterre*, environed with an easy agreeable *Slope* and proportionable Verges of Grass; adorn'd with *Apollo*, *Minerva* and *Pallas*, the *seven Liberal Arts*, *Mercury* and *Pytho*.

In the Center of this *Parterre* is an *octagon Basin of Water* which may be adorn'd with *Neptune*. This open Parterre is planted on the sides with double Lines of *Pines* and *Scotch Firs*. The *Terrace* with *Platanus*. The little Groves with *Lime Trees*. The open Grove with *Horse-Chesnuts*, and with *English Elm*. The middle or center excepted, which are Standards of *Scotch Firs*. The Avenue with *Platanus*: The Groves with Standards of *Holly*, *Yew*, *Bay Tree*, *Laurel*, *Ever-green*, *Oak*, *Box* and *Phillyrea*. All which Trees throughout these several Plantations are planted at their Bottoms, with *Honey Suckles*, *Sweet Briers*, *white Jessamine*, and the several Sorts of *Roses*: And about the Stem or Body of every Tree are cut Circles, about fourteen or sixteen Inches in Breadth sown with *Dwarf Stock*, *Candy Turf*, *Pinks*, *Sweet Williams*, *Catch-fly*, &c. which make no little Addition to the Beauty of our Plantations.

. . .

The *Serpentine*, and strait lined Walks within the Plantations of Wood or *Wilderness Work,* are planted with Standards of *Oak, Beach, Elm, Lime, Maple, Sycamore, Hornbeam, Birth, Platanus, Wicky* or *Quick-beam, Alder, Poplar, Withy,* and the *weeping* or *mourning Willow* that was brought in from *Babylon*, and now in great Plenty and Perfection in *England* . . .

The Hedges that are planted between the aforesaid Trees which form the Sides of the Walks are of *English, Dutch* and *French Elms, Lime, Hornbeam, Maple, Privet, Yew, Holly,*

Arbutus, Phillyrea, Norway Fir, Ilex, Bay, Laurel, Laurus-Tinus, Piracantha, Juniper and the *English Furze*: and indeed, a beautiful Plantation should not only be adorned with entire Walks and Hedges of Trees of all Sorts, as well Fruit as other; but intermix'd together in many parts, as if Nature had placed them there with her own hand.'

– *New Principles of Gardening* by Batty Langley (1728)

Walpole on the development of ha-has:

'The capital stroke, the leading step to all that has followed, was (I believe first thought was Bridgman's*) the destruction of walls for boundaries, and the invention of *fossès* – an attempt then deemed so astonishing, that the common people called them Ha! Ha's! to express their surprize at finding a sudden and unperceived check to their walk . . ..

I call a sunk fence the leading step, for these reasons. No sooner was this simple enchantment made, than levelling, mowing and rolling, followed. The contiguous ground of

---

* Although Charles Bridgeman, and indeed William Kent, were both early adopters of the ha-ha, the system was first used in France (where they were called 'ah-ahs') in *c.*1700.

the park without the sunk fence was to be harmonized with the lawn within; and the garden in its turn was to be set free from its prim regularity, that it might assort with the wilder country without. The sunk fence ascertained the specific garden, but that it might not draw too obvious a line of distinction between the neat and the rude, the contiguous out-lying parts came to be included in a kind of general design: and when nature was taken into the plan, under improvements, every step that was made, pointed out new beauties and inspired new ideas. At that moment appeared Kent, painter enough to taste the charms of the landscape, bold and opinionative enough to dare and to dictate, and born with a genius to strike out a great system from the twilight of imperfect essays. He leaped the fence, and saw that all nature was a garden. He felt the delicious contrast of hill and valley changing imperceptibly into each other, tasted the beauty of the gentle swell, or concave scoop, and remarked how loose groves crowned an easy eminence with happy ornament, and while they called in the distant view between their graceful stems, removed and extended the perspective by delusive comparison.'

– The History of the Modern Taste in Gardening
by Horace Walpole (1780)

$\mathcal{O}_n$ *ruins etc:*

'RUINS of buildings, artificially formed, are sometimes introduced in pleasure ground designs; such as broken bridges, decayed temples, and such like, in some remote and retired situation; and on which is introduced several sorts of woody plants, as Ivy, &c. which naturally grow or ascend upon buildings and ruins; and with Weeping-Willows, &c. growing in the ground near.

HERMITAGES, are solitary, humble buildings, constructed in some obscure or lonesome part of pleasure grounds, and formed either of roots of trees, rustic stone, or rock-work, &c. arched over at top, and generally with an arched entrance of irregular form; having one or more internal apartments, and is commonly either contrived on the side of some riding ground or eminence, or so artificially formed by covering it at top with mould and grass, as to

An artificial ruin.

form a sort of grassy knowl, &c. with a private entrance in one side.'

— *The Young Gardener's Best Companion* by S. Fullmer (1786)

Repton on Cobham Hall:

Cobham Hall is a medieval manor located in Kent. When the third Lord Darnley inherited the estate in 1747 he began to remodel the house and grounds. Humphry Repton was employed to rework the gardens in 1790, and here he writes about his improvements:

'This venerable pile is situated in a valley in the middle of a large park, and was formerly exposed to the cattle on every side, except towards the east, where a large walled garden intervened. The operations were begun by enveloping the whole of the premises in plantations, shrubberies, or gardens; and these, after the growth of twenty-five years, have totally changed the character of the place. The house is no longer a huge pile, standing naked on a vast grazing ground: its walls are enriched with roses and jasmines; its apartments are perfumed with odours from flowers surrounding it on every side: and the animals which enliven the landscape are not admitted as an annoyance. All around is neatness, elegance, and comfort; while the views of the park are improved by the rich foreground, over which they are seen from the terraces in the garden, or the elevated situation of the apartments.

On the whole, Cobham furnishes a striking example of artificial arrangement for convenience in the grounds, immediately adjoining the house, contributing to the natural advantages of its situation and scenery, and enriched by the most luxuriant foliage and verdure. The home views give a perfect idea of what a park ought to be, without affecting to be a forest; for although its extent of domain might warrant such character, there is a natural amenity in the face of the country, that is more beautiful than romantic, more habitable than wild; and though in the valleys the view is not enlivened by water, which in a chalk soil is not to be expected, yet from the elevated points of the park the two most important rivers of England, the Thames and Medway, form part of the distant prospect.'

— Fragments on the Theory and Practice of Landscape Gardening
by Humphry Repton (1816)

Thoughts on planting rock-work:

'There is much exercise of mind required in disposing plants on rock-work as there is in building the masses of stones together. In fact, the placing of the plants in positions not only to exhibit their own beauties and peculiarities, but to bring more visibly into view the forms and colours of the rocks, in all their natural irregularity, is a work demanding even more taste and skill than building up the stones.

Plants give animation to rock-work, and are suggestive of many a thought which the bare rocks could never impart. The depths of darkest shade should embrace within their stony folds plants of light coloured flowers or foliage, to relieve their gloom, and assist the eye in tracing out their intricate windings. *Cerastium Biebersteinii,* with its white leaves and whiter flowers, and procumbent habit of growth, is admirably adapted for such a purpose, either planted in a recess or suspended gracefully over the front of some stone. *Arabis procurrens* is also a beautiful plant for a like purpose, though less effective than the former, from its flowers being small and white, and its leaves green; still its close symmetrical character renders it very suitable for setting off some rough irregularly-formed stone. *Aubrieta purpurea grandiflora,* as its name implies, is a charming purple-flowering spring plant, differing from its congeners in its larger flowers, and will be seen to best advantage planted on some external or prominent part of the rock-work, where its colder-coloured flowers will bring forward the rocks; while the white-coloured flowers will add depth and extension to the view, and therefore heighten the irregularity of the whole. True to its nature, the eye demands the sunshine as well as the shade; and with our many-sided stones and differently-formed plants, as well as great variety of colour amongst flowers, it is in our power to meet the eye's requirements.'

> – 'Thoughts on Planting Rock-Work' by John Caie,
> Gardener to the Dowager Duchess of Bedford,
> Camden-hill, Kensington. Article from *Gardeners'
> Magazine of Botany: The Garden Companion
> and Florists' Guide*, April 1852

Jefferson on English gardens:

Thomas Jefferson with fellow future US President, John Adams, toured English gardens in April 1786. Jefferson was keen on both architecture and gardening and recorded his impressions of the English gardens he visited in *Notes of a Tour of English Gardens*:

'Memorandums made on a tour to some of the gardens in England described by Whately in his book on gardening. While his descriptions in point of style are models of perfect elegance and classical correctness, they are as remarkeable for their exactness. I always walked over the gardens with his book in my hand, examined with attention the particular spots he described, found them so justly characterised by him as to be easily recognised, and saw with wonder, that his fine imagination had never been able to seduce him from the truth. My enquiries were directed chiefly to such practical things as might enable me to estimate the expence of making and maintaining a garden in that style. My journey was in the months of March and April 1786.

Cheswick. Belongs to D. of Devonshire. Garden about 6. acres. The Octagonal dome has an ill effect, both within and without; the garden shews still too much of art; an obelisk of very ill effect. Another in the middle of a pond useless.

Hampton court. Old fashioned. Clipt yews grown wild.

Twickenham. Pope's original garden 3 ½ as. Sr. Wm. Stanhope added 1 ½ acre. This is a long narrow slope, grass and trees in the middle, walk all round. Now Sr. Wellbore Ellis's. Obelisk at bottom of Pope's garden as monument to his mother. Inscription. Ah! Edithe matrum optuma, mulierum amantissima, Vale. The house about 30. yds. from the Thames; the ground shelves gently to the water side. On the back of the house passes the street, and beyond that the garden. The grotto is under the street, and goes out level to the water. In the center of the garden a mound with a spiral walk round it. A rookery.

Esher place. The house in a bottom near the river. On the other side the ground rises pretty much. The road by which we come to the house forms a dividing line in the middle of the front. On the right are heights, rising one beyond and above another, with clumps of trees. On the farthest a temple. A hollow filled up with a clump of trees, the tallest in the bottom, so that the top is quite flat. On the left the ground descends. Clumps of trees. The clumps on each hand balance finely. A most lovely mixture of concave and convex. The garden is of about 45. as. besides the park which joins. Belongs to Lady Francis Pelham.

Claremont. Ld. Clive. Nothing remarkeable.

Paynshill. Mr. Hopkins. 323. as. garden and park all in one. Well described by Whately. Grotto said to have cost 7000.£. Whately says one of the bridges is of stone. But both are now of wood. The lower 60. f. high. There is too much evergreen. The Dwelling house built by Hopkins. Ill situated. He has not been there in 5. years. He lived there 4. years while building the present house. It is not finished. It's architecture is incorrect. A Doric temple beautiful.

Woburn. Belongs to Ld. Peters. Ld. Loughborough is the present tenant for 2. lives. 4. people to the farm. 4. to the pleasure garden. 4. to the kitchen garden. All are

A Doric temple.

intermixed, the pleasure garden being merely a highly ornamented walk through and round the divisions of the farm and kitchen garden.

Caversham. Sold by Ld. Cadogan to Majr. Marsac. 25. as. of garden, 400. as. of park, 6 as. of kitchen garden. A large lawn, separated by a sunk fence from the garden, appears to be part of it. A straight broad gravel walk passes before the front and parallel to it, terminated on the right by a Doric temple, and opening at the other end on a fine prospect. This straight walk has an ill effect. The lawn in front, which is pasture, well disposed with clumps of trees.

Wotton. Now belongs to the M. of Buckingham, son of George Grenville. The lake covers 50. as. the river 5. as. the bason 15. as. the little river 2. as. = 72. as. of water. The lake and great river are on a level. They fall into the bason 5. f. below, and that again into the little river 5. f. lower. These waters lie in form of an L. The house is in middle of open side, forming the angle. A walk goes round the whole,

3. miles in circumference, and containing within it about 300. as. Sometimes it passes close to the water, sometimes so far off as to leave large pasture ground between it and water. But 2. hands to keep the pleasure grounds in order. Much neglected. The water affords 2000. brace of carp a year. There is a Palladian bridge of which I think Whately does not speak.

Stowe. Belongs to the M. of Buckingham, son of G. Grenville, and who takes it from Ld. Temple. 15. men and 18. boys employed in keeping pleasure grounds. Within the Walk are considerable portions separated by inclosures and used for pasture. The Egyptian pyramid is almost entirely taken down by the late Ld. Temple to erect a building there, in commemoration of Mr. Pitt, but he died before beginning it, and nothing is done to it yet. The grotto, and two rotundas are taken away. There are 4. levels of water, receiving it one from the other. The bason contains 7. as. the lake below that 10. as. Kent's building is called the temple of Venus. The inclosure is entirely by ha! ha! At each end of the front line there is a recess like the bastion of a fort. In one of these is the temple of Friendship, in the other the temple of Venus. They are seen the one from the other, the line of sight passing, not thro' the garden, but through the country parallel to the line of the garden. This has a good effect. In the approach to Stowe, you are brought a mile through a straight avenue, pointing to the Corinthian arch and to the house, till you get to the Arch. Then you turn short to the right. The straight approach is very ill. The Corinthian arch has a very useless appearance, inasmuch as it has no pretension to any destination. Instead of being an object from the house, it is an obstacle to a very pleasing distant prospect. The Graecian valley being clear of trees, while the hill on each side is covered with them, is much deepened to appearance.

Leasowes. In Shropshire. Now the property of Mr. Horne by purchase. 150. as. within the walk. The waters small. This is not even an ornamented farm. It is only a grazing farm with a path round it. Here and there a seat of board, rarely any thing better. Architecture has contributed nothing. The obelisk is of brick. Shenstone had but 300£ a year, and ruined himself by what he did to this farm. It is said that he died of the heartaches which his debts occasioned him. The part next the road is of red earth, that on the further part grey. The 1st. and 2d. cascades are beautiful. The landscape at No. 18. and prospect at 32. are fine. The Walk through the wood is umbrageous and pleasing. The whole arch of prospect may be of 90°. Many of the inscriptions are lost.

Hagley. Now Ld. Wescot. 1000. as. No distinction between park and garden. Both blended, but more of the character of garden. 8. or 9. labourers keep it in order. Between 2. and 300. deer in it, some few of them red deer.

They breed sometimes with the fallow. This garden occupying a descending hollow between the Clent and Witchbury hills, with the spurs from those hills, there is no level in it for a spacious water. There are therefore only some small ponds. From one of these there is a fine cascade; but it can only be occasionally, by opening the sluice. This is in a small, dark, deep hollow, with recesses of stone in the banks on every side. In one of these is a Venus pudique, turned half round as if inviting you with her into the recess. There is another cascade seen from the Portico on the bridge. The castle is triangular, with a round tower at each angle, one only entire; it seems to be between 40. and 50. f. high. The ponds yield a great deal of trout. The walks are scarcely gravelled.

Blenheim. 2500. as. of which 200. is garden, 150. water, 12. kitchen garden, and the rest park. 200. people employed to keep it in order, and to make alterations and additions. About 50. of these employed in pleasure grounds. The turf is mowed once in 10. days, in summer. About 2000. fallow deer in the park, and 2. or 3000. sheep. The palace of H.2. was remaining till taken down by Sarah, widow of the 1st. D. of Marlborough. It was on a round spot levelled by art, near what is now water, and but a little above it. The island was a part of the high road leading to the palace. Rosamond's bower was near where is now a little grove about 200. yards from the palace. The well is near where the bower was. The water here is very beautiful, and very grand. The cascade from the lake a fine one. Except this the garden has no great beauties. It is not laid out in fine lawns and woods, but the trees are scattered thinly over the ground, and every here and there small thickets of shrubs, in oval raised beds, cultivated, and flowers among the shrubs. The gravelled walks are broad. Art appears too much. There are but a few seats in it, and nothing of architecture more dignified. There is no one striking position in it. There has been a great addition to the length of the river since Whately wrote.

Enfield chase. One of the 4. lodges. Garden about 60. as. originally by Ld. Chatham, now in the tenure of Dr. Beaver, who married the daughter of Mr. Sharpe. The lease lately renewed. Not in good repair. The water very fine. Would admit of great improvement by extending walks &c. to the principal water at the bottom of the lawn.

Moor-Park Lawn about 30. as. A piece of ground up the hill of 6. as. A small lake. Clumps of Spruce firs. Surrounded by walk separately inclosed. Destroys unity. The property of Mr. Rous, who bought of Sr. Thomas Dundas. The building superb. The principal front a Corinthian portico of 4. columns. In front of the wings a colonnade, Ionic, subordinate. Back front a terras, 4. Corinthian pilasters. Pulling down wings of building. Removing deer. Wants water.'

– Notes of a Tour of English Gardens
by Thomas Jefferson (1786)

On planting:

'The works of a person that builds, begins immediately to decay; while those of him who plants begin directly to improve. In this, planting promises a more lasting pleasure, than building; which, were it to remain in equal perfection, would at best begin to moulder and want repairs in imagination. Now trees have a circumstance that suits our taste, and that is annual variety. It is inconvenient indeed, if they cause our love of life to take root and flourish with them; whereas the very sameness of our structures will, without the help of dilapidation, serve to wean us from our attachment to them.'

— *The Works in Verse and Prose of*
William Shenstone (1777, 5th ed.)

On the division of a pleasure garden:

'A gentlemen who has a pleasure-garden, is to consider it under four articles, He is to have, 1. Hardy plants; and

2. Flowering shrubs; which stands all the year in the borders;
3. Tender annuals; which are to be raised in hot-beds, and brought into the common borders during summer; and,
4. Choice flowers which are produced in a nursery, and afterward planted in particular beds.

Of the first sort, or hardy plants, that stand the winter, are *Campanulas, French honeysuckles, Hollyhocks, Columbines, Sweet Williams, Wall-flowers,* and the like. These are to be raised from seed in a nursery, and brought into the garden the season before they are to flower.

Of the second kind, or shrubs, are *Roses, Honeysuckles, Lilac's,* or the like, which are to be raised from layers or cuttings, or from suckers, in the same nursery with the hardy plants.

Of the third kind, or tender annuals, are *French* and

Tulip.

African Marygolds, Balsams, Globe Amaranths, and *China-asters.* These are to be removed from one hot-bed to another, till the season growing warm, and they gathering strength, they are at length planted in the borders; and thrive as if they had been raised there from the first.

Of the fourth kind, or choice flowers, are *Auricula's, Carnations, Tulips, Anemones, Rannunculus's,* and the like. These are all perennial; and to have them in perfection, they must be raised from seed in a nursery, and in due time brought into the garden.

Under these four heads may be comprehended the whole practice of common gardening; and as each class of these has a particular course of culture, the business may accordingly be divided into four kinds: 1. The raising tender annuals on hot-beds in spring. 2. The raising hardy biennials or perennials in the nursery in open ground. 3. The management of choice and curious flowers: which differs no way from the former, but in that it requires more time and care: and, 4. The propagating trees and shrubs, by cuttings, layers, or suckers. He that knows how to do these four things, is qualified to take care of any common garden; and when he rightly understand the culture of one plant of either class, he will know to manage them all.'

– *The Practice of Gardening* by Thomas Perfect* (1759)

* Perfect was keen to debunk the mysteries of gardening and to move away from the idea that it was an amusement reserved for gentlemen gardeners, he explained of his own book: 'Books of gardening are tedious; and difficult to understand: and the best of them are very expensive . . . for this reason the present short account is published; which contains the whole without reserve, and is so plain that any body may understand it.'

On springs and water-works:

'I come now to treat of Water, in respect of that Beauty and Decorum it furnishes a Country Seat or *Villa* withal, some Directions for conveying it to the place 'tis to be us'd, the Method of making Canals, Ponds, Cascades, and Fountains . . ..

But whatever it be, Nature has dispos'd of Springs, generally speaking, on the Sides of Hills, to our great Advantage, since by that means they may be easily convey'd to what Place the Ingenious Designer thinks fit: And considering how beautiful an Addition Water is to Gard'ning, 'tis hardly to be purchas'd too dear, being indeed the Life and Spirit of all Country Seats, without which they are dull and flat . . .. I am not altogether against Fountains adorn'd with Masonry, and other superficial Embellishments, but cann't advise them in any but in the most elegant Quarters and Recesses of what we esteem the finest Part of the Gardens.'

— *The Nobleman, Gentleman, and Gardener's Recreation*
by Stephen Switzer (1715)

On maintaining water features:

'Water, whether as an ornamental feature, or as an aquarium, should be kept clear both of weeds and insects. Of aquatic weeds the most troublesome in small aquariums are the confervae and byssi, which can only be removed by hand, or by entangling them with a rake or broom. The larvae of numerous land insects are deposited in water or in the muddy sides of ponds and ditches, as the elephant-hawk-moth (*Sphinx Elpenor*, L.), the dragonfly (*Libellula*, L.), and many others. Of the aquatic kinds are the well known tipulae, of which some species (*T. oleracea*) glide over the water, and are by many considered rather ornamental than otherwise, and others live entirely under it, and feed on the roots of plants. To destroy or at least greatly to keep under all aquatic insects, an effectual mode is to dry the pond for a day or two; but in the case of an aquarium it cannot be done; fish and frogs, their natural enemies, must therefore be encouraged, in order that they may attack them.'

– An Encyclopaedia of Gardening; Comprising the Theory and Practice of Horticulture, Floriculture, Arboriculture, and Landscape-Gardening by J. C. Loudon (1822)

Elephant-hawk-moth.

Price on the picturesque in water:

'But among all the objects of nature, there is none in which roughness and smoothness more strongly mark the distinction between the two characters, than in water. A calm, clear lake, with the reflections of all that surrounds it, seen under the influence of a setting sun, at the close of an evening clear and serene as its own surface, is, perhaps, of all scenes, the most congenial to our ideas of beauty in its strictest and in its most general sense.

Nay, though the scenery around should be the most wild and picturesque (I might almost say the most savage) every thing is so softened and melted together by the reflection of such a mirror, that the prevailing idea, even then, might possibly be that of beauty, so long as the water itself was chiefly regarded. On the other hand, all water whose surface is broken, and whose motion is abrupt and irregular, as universally accords with our ideas of the picturesque; and whenever the word is mentioned, rapid and stony torrents and cataracts, and the waves dashing against rocks, are among the first images that present themselves to our imagination. The two characters also approach and balance each other, as roughness or smoothness, as gentle undulation or abruptness prevail.'

— *An Essay on the Picturesque* by Uvedale Price, 1796

On gardening jobs for May:

'May. Gemini, or the Twins.

Begin to graft in this Month, according as you find the Buds ready, which take off the Middle of your Sprouts. Fetch out your Greens and Transplant them into Boxes filled with Good Earth, mixed with one part of rotten Cow-dung, putting Sticks or light Rubbish to make the Earth lie light; so make a Hole for the Water at the bottom; then set your Plants therein, but not deep; water them and set them on the Sun.'

— *The Gentleman's, Traveller's, Husbandman's and Gardener's Pocket Companion* (1751)

Defoe on Chatsworth:

Daniel Defoe's account of his travels throughout Great Britain were published in three volumes 1724–27, and were extremely popular – his most profitable work in his lifetime after *Robinson Crusoe*. Among his many colourful observations is his impression of Chatsworth:

'First, 'tis to be observed that on the East Side rises a very high Mountain, on the top of which they dig Mill-stones, and it begins so close to, and so overlooks the house, being prodigiously high that, should they roll down a pair of those stones couple with a wooden Axis, as is the way of drawing them, they would infallibly give a Shock to the Building; yet this Mountain is so planted, and so covered with a Wood of beautiful Trees, that you see no Hill, only a rising Wood, as if the trees grew so much higher than one another, and was only a wall of Trees, whose tops join into one another so close, as nothing is seen through them.

Upon the top of that Mountain begins a vast extended Moor or Waste, which, for fifteen or sixteen miles together due North, presents you with neither Hedge, House or Tree, but a waste and housing Wilderness, over which when strangers travel, they are obliged to take Guides, or it would be impossible not to lose their way.

Nothing can be more surprising of its Kind, than for a Stranger coming from the North, suppose from Sheffield in

Chatsworth House and its grounds, mid-eighteenth century.

Yorkshire, for that is the first Town of Note, and wandering or labouring to pass this difficult Desart Country, and seeing no End of it, and almost discouraged and beaten out with the Fatigue of it, (just such was our Case) on a sudden the Guide brings him to this Precipice, where he looks down from a frightful height, and a comfortless, barren, and, as he thought, endless Moor, into the most delightful Valley, with the most pleasant Garden, and most beautiful Palace in the World: If contraries illustrate, and the place can admit of any illustration, it must needs add to the Splendour of the Situation, and to the Beauty of the Building, and I must say (with which I will close my short Observation) if there is any Wonder in *Chatsworth*, it is, That any Man who had a Genius suitable to so magnificent a Design, who could lay out the Plan for such a House, and had a Fund to support the Charge, would build it in such a Place where the Mountains insult the Clouds, intercept the Sun, and would threaten, *were Earthquakes frequent here*, to bury the very Towns, much more the House, in their Ruins.'

– A Tour Thro' The Whole Island of Great Britain
by Daniel Defoe (1724–27)

On the pleasure ground and flower garden:

'A General Pleasure Ground, being a grand district of gardening, appropriated wholly for pleasure, amusement, observation, and as a principal ornament to a country seat; is composed of spacious grass lawns, elegant plantations, ornamental walks, pieces of water, &c. diversified in a curious representation of art and nature, so artfully varied in the general scene, that new varieties continually present themselves in the excursion through the different compartments; consisting of ornamental tree plantations and shrubberies; comprising beautiful flowering shrubs and evergreens, and compartments of elegant flowers: comprehending not only the space within the limits of the garden, but all ornamental plantations extended to any adjacent out-grounds, parks, paddocks, &c. may be considered as appertaining to the pleasure ground.

Modern pleasure grounds are so planned in their design, as to exhibit a grand imitation of nature: discovering at first entrance a spacious grass lawn, bounded by irregular clumps and groves of tree and shrub plantations, with serpentine walks winding through them, having the internal parts also formed into grand opens, spacious walks, and clumps and thickets of shrubs, trees and flowers, in rural sweeps of various dimensions.'

– *The Young Gardener's Best Companion* by S. Fullmer (1786)

Planting sweet-smelling flowers:

'In the twelve Months of the Year, there are eight which will produce Flower, both grateful to the Eye, and pleasant to the Smell; as

In *January*, the several Kinds of Polyanthos

In *February*, the Polyanthos, Hyacinths, and Violets.

In *March*, the Polyanthus, Hyacinths, Stock July-Flowers, and Violets, Roses, if against a South Wall.

In *April*, the Hyacinths, Stock July-Flowers, Wall-Flowers, Auriculas, Junquils, Roses, white Narcissus, and Narcissus Polyanthos.

In *May*, the Wall-Flowers, white Nar-cissus, Lillies, and double flower'd Rocket, Roses.

In *June*, the Sweet William, Lillies, Primrose Tree, Pinks, Rose, and Carnations.

Primrose.

In *July*, the Sweet William, Pinks, Carnation, and Tuberose, and lastly,

In *August*, the Pink, and July-Flowers, commonly called Carnations.

The Odours of these Flowers being extreamly pleasant, are therefore to be planted in every Walk, and of each an equal Quantity; that thereby they may always be adorn'd with one or other according to their natural Succession.'

— *New Principles of Gardening* by Batty Langley (1728)

On gardening:

' . . . Where ev'ry muse her grateful tribute brought,
And Virtue practis'd what sound Learning taught:
At length her longing eyes and hallow'd feet
Reach'd verdant STOWE's magnificent retreat,
Where fame and truth had promis'd, she should find
Scenes to improve and please her curious mind:
Each step invention, elegance display'd,
Such, as when Churchill woes the Aonian maid,
And joins in easy graceful negligence,
Th' harmonius powers of verse, with sterling sense:
Such, as when Poussin's or Albano's hand,
On glowing canvas the rich landscape plann'd,

And classic genius strove by mimic art,
Thro' the admiring eye to reach the heart.
Amidst the wonders of each striking scene,
High on the summit of a sloping green,
A solemn Temple, in proportion true,
Magnificently simple, courts the view;
CONCORD and VICTORY with pride proclaim
This mansion sacred to Britannia's fame,
Whose form majestic from all hands receives
The various product ev'ry region gives;
Pleas'd at her feet their choicest gifts to lay,
And homage to her power superior pay;
The sculptur'd walls her glories past declare,
In proud memorials of successful war;
No factious sacrifice to France and Spain
These consecrated trophies can profane;
For Public Liberty her awful seat
Here fixing, here protects her last retreat;
Where to the great and good in every shade,
The fragrant tribute of just praise is paid;
Where the prime beauties, form'd by Nature's hand
Throughout her works in every distant land,
Transplanted, flourish in their native ease,
And, as by magic charm collected, please –
Here the fair queen of this heroic isle,
Imperial Albion, with a gracious smile

Confess'd, she lovely nature saw, at last,
Unite with art, and both improve by taste.'

— Stowe: A Description of the House and Gardens
by Thomas Medland (1817)

On flower maintenance:

'The cutting off flower-stalks, decaying flowers, leaves, &c.
is to be done in most cases immediately after the flowers
are faded; but there are exceptions where the leaves on the
lower part of flower-stems may be requisite to strengthen
the root, and where, as in the case of stipa, some conval-
larias, eringoes, &c. the parts of the flower are persisting, or
the fruit or seed-pods are objects of beauty. The leaves of
bulbous-rooted plants, and such others as are not prolific
in foliage, should be carefully preserved till they have begun
to decay; and, indeed, the base or root-leaves of no plant
whatever should be cut off till this is the case, unless for
some particular object. Every single flower, as soon as the
petals begin to droop, should be pinched off, and especially
every flower of the double kind. Every rose, when it begins
to droop, should be clipt off near to the footstalk of the

one which is about to succeed it; and when the last of the corymb has done flowering, then the common foot-stalk should be cut off back to the first strong leaf-bud: nothing is more unsightly in a flower-garden than rose-bushes where this has not been attended to. By employing women or apprentices to go over the whole pleasure-ground every morning during the four summer months, to attend to this business, it may be completely accomplished at very little expense. These and other points of management, we know, are considered needless niceties by many gardeners: but what is a flower-garden unless it is kept with the utmost nicety? Others will tell you, they have not time for such things; but where there is a real taste for neatness, time will be found. "No gentleman," Sir G. Mackenzie observes, "ought to keep a gardener who does not understand that there is time enough for every thing, provided that time is not wasted, but properly regulated, and nothing too long delayed."'

– An Encyclopaedia of Gardening; Comprising the Theory and Practice of Horticulture, Floriculture, Arboriculture, and Landscape-Gardening by J. C. Loudon (1822)

On gravel:

'GRAVEL and *Grass* are natural Ornaments to a Country-Seat, and are the Glory of the *English* Gardens, and Things by which we excel all other Nations, as *France*, *Holland*, *Flanders*, &c.

There are different Sorts of *Gravel*; but for those who can conveniently have it, I approve of that *Gravel* on *Black-Heath* as preferable to most that we have in *England*, it consisting of smooth even Pebbles, which, when mix'd with a due Quantity of Loam, will bind exceedingly close and look very beautiful, and continue handsome longer than any other sort of *Gravel* which I have yet seen.'

– *The Gardeners Dictionary* by Philip Miller (1737)

On shrubberies:

'*Shrubberies* and *beds of flowers* demand limitation: – immoderately extended, they mark the triumph of luxury over elegance. The apparent waste of ground displeases us; and the plants themselves are too minute to have any considerable space exclusively allotted to them. (I say this, in regard to *beauty of disposition*, and mean not to interfere with the *vanity of collections*.) On spots, that have nothing observable in themselves, such profusion of ornament is generally bestowed; yet, however fashionably patronized, gaudy colouring is a poor compensation for natural deficiencies.'

– An Essay on Design in Gardening
by George Mason (1768)

On planting the shrubbery:

'On planting the shrubbery the same general remarks, submitted as introductory to planting the flower-garden, are applicable; and shrubs may be arranged in as many different manners as flowers. Trees, however, are permanent and conspicuous objects, and consequently produce an effect during winter, when the greater number of herbaceous plants are scarcely visible. This is more especially the case

Mulberry tree.

with that class called evergreens, which, according as they are employed or omitted, produce the greatest difference in the winter aspect of the shrubbery. . . . Before proceeding farther it is requisite to observe, that the proportion of evergreen trees to deciduous trees in cultivation in this country, is as 1 to 12; of evergreen shrubs to deciduous shrubs, exclusive of climbers and creepers but including roses, as 4 to 8; that the time of the flowering of trees and shrubs is from March to August inclusive, and that the colors of the flowers are the same as in herbaceous plants. These data will serve as guides for the selection of species and varieties for the different modes of arrangement, but more especially for the mingled manner.

– *An Encyclopaedia of Gardening; Comprising the Theory and Practice of Horticulture, Floriculture, Arboriculture, and Landscape-Gardening* by J. C. Loudon (1822)

On where gardeners should live:

'Sir,

I have lately purchased your excellent work, the Encyclopedia of Gardening, and also the Gardener's Magazine, both of which are exceedingly useful, more particularly to gardeners at a distance from the metropolis. Indeed such a work as the Magazine has been wanted of late, and I hope will be well supported by gardeners; and I am happy, Sir, that in the above works you have so well pointed out the moral and religious duties of gardeners, with almost all other acquirements belonging to their profession, to all of which I coincide with you; but permit me, Sir, to enquire whether the gardener in England, placed, as he is, in the housekeeper's room, – I say, whether he can improve himself? I answer, – all that he can do there, admitting it to be an improvement, is, – he may read a little, play at cards, dance, and flirt with ladies' maids. But in some families of the first rank and respectability, the gardener is, as is the case at present with myself, a servants' hall inmate. Now, I ask again, Sir, as in the former case, in what way is a gardener to improve himself there? Why, if he is a hail fellow, well met, with the inmates of this last apartment, his improvements are entirely out of the question; his amusements, or rather, his degradation, is hard at hand, – as drinking, swearing, and low language, is as much to be found in such a place, generally speaking, as in the *ale-house*.

There are many gentlemen, when hiring their gardeners, wish them to sleep in the house, to protect their property in the absence of the family; would it not be much better, where there is extensive gardens, with forcing houses, &c., for the superintendent of such to be placed in or as near to them as possible? But it requires no more common sense to see the absurdity of any other arrangement than that of a proper house for a head gardener in the garden, where at least extensive forcing of any kind is carried on: for instead of this being an expence, as gentlemen may think it to be, it will be found quite the reverse; for the man who takes delight in gardening will then be on the spot, where his chief business lies, without trusting to unexperienced hands, which is often the case with those placed in such circumstances as above described; and gardeners are often led away by servants and lose their places, more through this than any other circumstance.

Having Sir, intruded thus far in your notice, I hope and trust that you and your numerous correspondents will endeavour to impress on the minds of noblemen and gentlemen the evil effects of placing their gardeners any where else but in their garden.

I am, Sir, &c.

A Common Sense reforming Gardener'

– Letter of 2 February 1826, submitted to and published in *The Gardener's Magazine* by J. C. Loudon (1826)

On symmetry:

'In the modern, or irregular, style of landscape gardening, as well as in the irregular style of architecture, which,
whether under the name of Gothic or Italian, is the style
of country houses now most prevalent, the production of
a whole requires a much greater knowledge of art than
in the ancient style, either of landscape-gardening, or of
Greek or Roman domestic architecture: in both these styles
an attempt was seldom made to produce a whole, except
by means of regularity and symmetry. It is almost unnecessary to state, that in the ancient style, whether in ground,
in wood, in water, or in buildings of every description, and
in roads, regularity or symmetry were the governing principles. The place, as a whole, was generally symmetrical,
one half reflecting the other; and the details were always
regular. In an age where beauties of irregularity, and the
variety produced by wild scenery, prevailed throughout
the country, those of regularity and symmetry would be
found to be characteristic of art and civilisation; and they
were preferred by our ancestors, with a taste as just and correct relatively to them, and to the circumstances in which
they were placed, as our widely differing taste is to us, and
our circumstances.

. . .

Now, in every pleasing landscape it will be found, that, if it were bisected perpendicularly by an imaginary line, something like an equal body of scenery would be found on each side. The same may be said with reference to any irregular building which is pleasing as a picture, and also to any irregular flower-garden, or the planting of an irregular park. A pleasure-ground, which, viewed from the drawingroom [sic] windows, appeared to have all the shrubs on one side, and only flowers and lawn on the other, would not be so satisfactory as one where they were more equally balanced.'

— *The Suburban Gardener and Villa Companion*
by J. C. Loudon (1838)

Of the general culture and management of the flower-garden and shrubbery:

'The cultivation of the flower-garden is simple compared with that of the kitchen garden, both from its limited extent and the general sameness of its products; but to manage it to perfection requires a degree of nicety and constant attention beyond any other open-air department of gardening. As the stalks of flowering plants shoot up, they generally require thinning, and props for support; and the blossom, both of plants and shrubs,

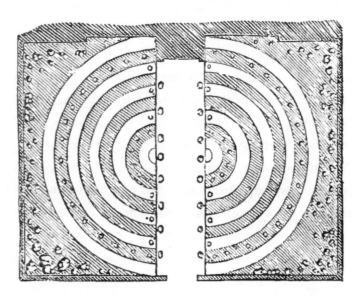

Flower garden design as an entrance to a house.

no sooner expands than it begins to wither, and must be cut off, unless, as in some of the ornamental shrubs, they are left for the sake of the beauty of their fruit.

Weeding, watering, stirring the soil, cutting off stems which have done flowering, attending to grass and gravel, must go hand in hand with these operations.'

> *– An Encyclopaedia of Gardening; Comprising the Theory and Practice of Horticulture, Floriculture, Arboriculture, and Landscape-Gardening* by J. C. Loudon (1822)

Creating shady walks of trees:

'SHADY WALKS of TREES, for shady and private walking, are occasionally introduced, both in continued plantations of trees, either closely planted in the manner of thickets or woods, or as groves, shrubberies, &c. towards, or around the out-boundary of the pleasure ground, or along those adjoining spacious lawns; allotting proper spaces for the walks, which should either be gravel or sand, or grass, occasionally; or may form shady walks, by planting detached close ranges of trees, or trees and shrubs together, on each side of the walk, which may occasionally be both in the serpentine order and straight; planting the tree kinds and taller shrubs behind, and the lowest next the walk; having the rows of trees on the opposite sides of the walk, planted only at such distances, row from row, as to afford the proper shade required.'

— *The Young Gardener's Best Companion* by S. Fullmer (1786)

Price on the picturesque in trees:

'Among trees, it is not the smooth young beech, or the fresh and tender ash, but the rugged old oak, or knotty wych elm, that are picturesque; nor is it necessary they should be of great bulk; it is sufficient if they are rough, mossy, with a character of age, and with sudden variations in their forms. The limbs of huge trees, shattered by lightning or tempestuous winds, are in the highest degree picturesque; but whatever is caused by those dreaded powers of destruction, must always have a tincture of the sublime.'

– *An Essay on the Picturesque* by Uvedale Price, 1796

On gardening jobs for June:

'June. Cancer, or the Crab.

In this Month, water new planted Trees, and put rotten Fern about their Stems. Inoculate Apples, Pear, Wall Fruit, &c. Lop off needless Branches from your Vines, and stop the Joints. Gather Herbs to keep in the Full of the Moon; you may again sow Radish, Lettuce and Chervil.'

– *The Gentleman's, Traveller's, Husbandman's and Gardener's Pocket Companion* (1751)

Gilpin on the Leasowes:

'Few places had raised our expectations more than the Leasowes. So great a lover of nature as Mr. Shenstone appears to be in his writings, could not possibly, one would imagine, deviate from her in any of the operations of his genius. I shall give the reader a slight sketch of the scene; and then make a few general observations.

We entered the ground, (which contain about a hundred acres) by a wicket, near the bottom of a lane, which leads to the house. We should have been carried first into the higher parts; where we might have had a view of the whole at once. We should then have seen that it is, what is properly called, an *adorned farm*; and should have taken that idea along with us. The fields lie about the house; and a walk leads you round them.

We entered however below the house; and were carried first into a narrow, woody valley: from which emerging, we had a pleasant opening into the country about Hale's-Owen.

From this view we dip into a woody bottom, where we find Melibeus's seat, a sequestered spot, proper for the noon-tide retreat of a shepherd, and his flock.

From hence we penetrate another wood, and come suddenly on a long succession of waterfalls (fourteen of them) seen through an irregular vista of trees. The scenery is whimsical but amusing.

View of LEASOWES near Halesowen in SHROPSHIRE, including the Priory & Seat of the late Will.m Shenstone Esq.r

Engraving of The Leasowes, 1779.

Having thus traversed the lower ground, the path leads into the higher; and we begin now to discover, that it is carrying us round the whole. Here we have distant views, bounded by the Wrekin in Shropshire.

From these grounds the path makes a sudden dip to a sequestered vale, where Mr. Shenstone has dedicated an urn to the memory of a beloved lady. From hence it rises again, in a troublesome zig-zag, into the *Lover's walk*; which terminates, (oddly enough,) in the *temple of Pan*. With more propriety it might have led to the *temple of Hymen*.

From hence we descend again, through hanging fields, quite unadorned, to the most finished scene of the whole. It is a grove, ornamented at the upper end, by a cascade, from which the stream plays in irregular meanders among the trees; and passing under a romantic bridge, forms itself into a small lake. This whimsical spot is dedicated, I think, with some impropriety, to Virgil's genius; and is one of those ambiguous passages, which we are at a loss, whether to blame, or to commend. From hence we pass again into the lane, where we at first entered.

Tho Mr. Shenstone has, on the whole, shewn great taste and elegance, and has diversified his views very much; and been particularly happy in (that most agreeable mode of design,) affixing some peculiar character to each scene; yet in some things he has perhaps done *too much*; and in others *not enough*.

In the use of water he has been too profuse. He collects it only from a few springs, which ouze from his swampy grounds. It was a *force therefore on nature*, to attempt either a *river*, or a *lake*. A cascade, or a purling rill, should have satisfied his ambition. Besides, like the water of all swamps, the water of Leasowes wants brilliancy. Frothed by a fall, or quick descent, the impurities are less observed: in gentle motion they are striking; but in a lake they are offensive. It was ridiculous to see Naiads invited, by inscriptions, to bath their beauteous limbs in *crystal* pools, which stood before the eye, impregnated with all the filth which generates from stagnation.

He has done *too much* also in adorning his grounds so profusely with urns, statues, and buildings; which are commonly the most expensive, and least beautiful parts of improvement. In the *adorned farm* at least they *improper* decorations.

With his inscriptions, (in which many people say, he has done *too much* also) I own, I was pleased. When inscriptions are well-written, and properly adapted, as these generally are, they raise some leading thought; and impress the character of the scene in stronger ideas, than our own.

In other things Mr. Shenstone has perhaps done *too little*.

He might have thrown down more of his hedges: or, if that had been inconvenient, he might at least have concealed his inclosures more in plantations. His path on the *higher grounds*, is, in general, too open; and his foregrounds are often *regular fields*. This regularity might have been *disguised*.

The distances too would have appeared to more advantage, if they had sometimes been *over* a wood; and sometimes *through* an opening in one; or occasionally through the interstices among the boles of the trees.

But Mr. Shenstone's great deficiency lay in not draining, and clearing his grounds. If he had made his verdure richer, tho at the expense of his buildings, he had shewn a purer taste. But Shenstone was poor; and with a little of that vanity, which often attends poverty, he chose rather to lay out his money on what made the most shew, than on what would have been most becoming. From what he has done however, it is easy to conceive what he could have done; if he had a country suited to his ideas; and a fortune sufficient to adorn it.'

— *Observations on the Mountains and Lakes of Cumberland and Westmoreland* by William Gilpin (1786)

The character of oaks:

'All trees have a character analogous to that of men: Oaks are in all respects the perfect image of the manly character: In former times I should have said, and in present times I think I am authorised to say, the British one. As a brave man is not suddenly either elated by prosperity or depressed by adversity, so the oak displays not it's verdure on the sun's first approach; nor drops it, on his first departure. Add to this it's majestic appearance, the rough grandeur of it's bark, and the wide protection of it's branches.

A large, branching, aged oak, is perhaps the most venerable of all inanimate objects.'

– The Works in Verse and Prose of
William Shenstone (1777, 5th ed.)

Repton on the position of the kitchen garden:

'In the middle of the last century almost every mansion in the kingdom had its Garden, surrounded by walls, in the front of the house. To improve the landscape from the windows, Brown was obliged to remove those gardens; and not always being able to place them near the house, they were sometimes removed to a distance. This inconvenient part of his system has been most implicitly copied by his followers; although I observe that at Croome and some other places, where he found it practicable, he attached the kitchen garden to the offices and stables, &c. behind the mansion, surrounding the whole with a shrubbery; and indeed such an arrangement is most natural and commodious. The intimate connexion between the kitchen and the garden for its produce, and between the stables and the garden for its manure, is so obvious, that every one must see the propriety of bringing them as nearly together as possible, consistent with the views from the house.'

– Fragments on the Theory and Practice of Landscape Gardening
by Humphry Repton (1816)

On planting groves:

'In forming of groves, may have trees of various kinds; but should generally prefer those of the most handsome and lofty growth, and regular spreading heads, both of the deciduous and evergreen tribe; but have each of these planted in separate groves, or there may be groves or rows of different trees separately, as Elm groves, Lime Tree groves, and groves or separate rows of Chesnuts, Horse-Chesnuts, Walnuts, Beeches, Oak, Plane Tree, Maples, Larches, Poplars, Willow, Alder, &c. or all of these in one grove, for the greater variety: and of evergreens, there may be Pine, Fir, and Cedar groves, Evergreen Oak, Laurel, Cypress, &c. or a grove of all of these, and other lofty evergreens, will form a pleasing variety.

In procuring trees for groves, let them generally be such as are already somewhat advanced in growth, being of from five to six to eight or ten feet height, that they may at once make some tolerable appearance.'

– *The Young Gardener's Best Companion* by S. Fullmer (1786)

Of rural and extensive gardening:

'Rural and extensive gardening is naturally connected with a taste for planting *forest trees*; and an idea of the *picturesque* should ever accompany the work of planting. Merely for the sake of *objects* to gratify the *eye*, planting is very often pursued, and wherever trees can be introduced to improve a view from the *house*, or accustomed walks, *there* a man, having it in his power, as proprietor of the land, ought certainly to plant.

If to planting in *clumps, coppices, groves, avenues,* and *woods,* be added levelling of ground, improving of water courses, and pastures, making lawns, &c. the expence incurred would be *honourable,* and answered by pleasures of the sincerest kind! There are ways of spending money, that *could* be named, which are found mischievous in the extreme, and are therefore deservedly branded with disgrace; but he who

Planting trees; irregular placements with and without undergrowth.

distributes wealth into the hands of *industry,* working to useful purposes, and that delectable end of making a country
about him a *garden,* does so in wisdom.'

— *A Plain and Easy Introduction to the Knowledge and Practice
of Gardening* by Charles Marshall (1800)

Repton on the fashion of planting drives:

'I shall endeavour to trace the progress of fashion in
Planting; by which I mean the various systems adopted at
different periods for making trees artificial ornaments. The
first was doubtless that of planting them in a single row at

equal distances; and this prevailed in the gardens mentioned by Pliny.

The next step was in doubling these straight rows, to form shady walks; but fashion, not content with the simplicity of such an avenue of trees placed opposite to each other, invented the *Quincunx*, by which those straight lines were multiplied in three different directions.

As the eagerness of adopting this fashion could not always wait the tedious growth of trees, where old woods existed, they were cut through in straight lines and vistas, and in form of stars and *Pates d'oie**, which prevailed at the beginning of the last century.

Fashion, tired of the dull uniformity of straight lines, was then driven to adopt something new: yet still acting by geometrical rules, it changed to regular forms of circles and curves, in which the trees were always placed at equal distances. This introduced the serpentine avenue for a road . . ..

The next bold effort of fashion was that of departing from the equi-distant spaces, and trees were planted in patches of clumps, square or round, alternately shewing and hiding the view on each side of the road; and where no view was required, a screen or double row of trees entirely shut

---

* A pattern of pathways with three, four or five straight paths leading out from a central point, like a goose's foot, which was popular in French formal gardens.

out one side, while in the other the view was occasionally admitted, but still at regular intervals . . ..

About this time a total change in the fashion took place; and under Brown we were taught that Nature was to be our model, and that Nature seldom moved in a straight line. It was not therefore to be wondered at, that his illiterate followers should have copied the means he used, and not the model he proposed. They saw him prefer curved lines, and concluded that Nature abhorred a straight one. Hence proceeded those meandering, serpentine, and undulating lines in all their works, which were unfortunately confirmed by Hogarth's recommendation of his *imaginary Line of Beauty*. Thus we see roads sweeping round to avoid the direct line to their object, and fences gracefully and fancifully taking a longer course; and even belts and plantations in useless curves, with a drive meandering in parallel lines, which are full as much out of nature as straight ones.'

— Fragments on the Theory and Practice of Landscape Gardening
by Humphry Repton (1816)

General directions for creating a rural garden:

'I. THAT the grand Front of a Building lie open upon an elegant Lawn or Plain of Grass, adorn'd with beautiful Statues, (of which hereafter in the Place,) terminated on its Sides with open Groves.

II. That grand Avenues be planted from such large open Plains, with a Breadth proportionable to the Building, as well as to its Length of View.

III. That Views in Gardens be as extensive as possible.

IV. That such Walks, whose Views cannot be extended, terminate in Woods, Forests, misshapen Rocks, strange Precipices, Mountains, old Ruins, grand Buildings, &c.

V. That no regular Ever-Greens, &c. be planted in any Part of an open Plain or Parterre.

VI. That no Border be made, or Scroll-Work cut, in any such Lawn or plain Parterre; for the Grandeur of those beautiful Carpets consists in their native Plainess.

VII. That all Gardens be grand, beautiful, and natural.

VIII. That shady Walks be planted from the End-Views of a House, and terminate in those open Groves that enclose the Sides of the plain Parterre, that thereby you may enter into immediate Shade, as soon as out of the House, without being heated by the scorching Rays of the Sun.

IX. That all the Trees of your shady Walks and Groves be planted with Sweet-Brier, White Jessamine, and Honey-Suckles, environ'd at Bottom with a small Circle of Dwarf-Stock, Candy-Turf, and Pinks.

X. That all those Parts which are out of View from the House, be form'd into Wildernesses, labyrinths, &c.'

– *New Principles of Gardening* by Batty Langley (1728)

Beauty and character in the garden:

'Whatever contributes to render the scenes of nature delightful, is amongst the subjects of gardening; and animate, as well as inanimate objects, are circumstances of beauty or character. Several of these have been occasionally mentioned; others will readily occur; and nothing is unworthy of the attention of a gardener, which can tend to improve his compositions, whether by immediate effects, or by suggesting a train of pleasing ideas. The whole range of nature is open to him, from the parterre to the forest; and whatever is agreeable to the senses or the imagination, he may appropriate to the spot he is to improve: it is a part of his business to collect into one place, the delights which are generally dispersed through different species of country.

But in this application, the genius of the place must always be particularly considered; to force it is hazardous;

and an attempt to contradict it is always unsuccessful. The beauties peculiar to one character, cannot be transferred to its opposite; even where the characters are the same, it is difficult to copy directly from one into the other; and by endeavouring to produce a resemblance of a scene which is justly admired, the proper advantages of the place are often neglected for an imitation much inferior to the original . . . the art of gardening therefore is not to be studied in those spots only where it has been exercised; though they are in this country very numerous, and very various; yet all together they contain but a small proportion of the beauties which nature exhibits; and unless the gardener has stored his mind with ideas, from the infinite variety of the country at large, he will feel the want of that number, which is necessary for choice; he will have none ready to apply to the subject immediately before him; and will be reduced to copy an imitation. But improved places are of singular use to direct the judgment in the choice, and the combinations of the beauties in nature: an extensive knowledge of them is to be acquired in the country where they casually occur; discernment of their excellencies, and a taste for the disposition of them, is to be formed in places where they have been selected, and arranged with design.'

— *Observations on Modern Gardening*
by Thomas Whately (1770)

Price on Brown's made water:

'Of all the effects in landscape, the most brilliant and captivating are those produced by water, (as I have been told,)
Mr. Brown particularly piqued himself. If those beauties in
natural rivers and lakes which are imitable by art, and the
selections of them in the works of great painters, are the
best guides in forming artificial ones, Mr. Brown grossly
mistook his talent; for among all his tame productions, his
pieces of made water are perhaps the most so.

One of the most striking aspects of water, and that
which most distinguishes it from the grosser element of
earth, is its being a mirror that gives a peculiar freshness
and tenderness to the colours it reflects; it softens the
stronger lights, though the lucid veil it throws over them
seems hardly to diminish their brilliancy; it gives breadth to
the shadows, and in many cases a greater depth, while its
glassy surface preserves, and seems even to encrease their
transparency . . ..

In Mr. Brown's naked canals, nothing detains the eye
a moment; and the two bare sharp extremities appear to
cut into each other. If a near approach to mathematical
exactness were a merit instead of a defect, the sweeps of

Mr. Brown's water would be admirable; for many of them seem not to have been formed by degrees with spades, but scooped out at once by an immense iron crescent, which, after cutting out the indented part on one side, was applied to the opposite side, and then reversed to make the sweeps . . . where these pieces of water are made, if there happens to be any sudden breaks or inequalities in the ground; any thickets or bushes; any thing, in short, that might cover the rawness and formality of new work – instead of taking advantage of such accidents, all must be made level and bare; and, by a strange perversion of terms, stripping nature stark-naked, is called dressing her.'

– An Essay on the Picturesque by Uvedale Price, 1796

ℛepton on planting trees:

'It is difficult to lay down rules for any system of planting, which may ultimately be useful to this purpose; time, neglect, and accident, will often produce unexpected beauties. The gardener or nurseryman makes his holes at equal distance, and generally in straight rows; he then fills the holes with plants, and carefully avoids putting two of the same sort near each other; nor is it very easy to make him ever

Fragments of hedgerow.

put two or more trees into the same hole, or within a yard of each other: he considers them as cabbages or turnips, which will rob each other's growth, unless placed at equal distances; although in forests we most admire those double trees or thick clusters, whose stems seem to rise from the same root, entangled with the roots of thorns and bushes in every direction.'

    – *An Enquiry into the Changes of taste in Landscape Gardening*
by H. Repton (1806)

A letter on the Leasowes:

'The moment I entered this quiet and sequestered valley, the superlative genius of Shenstone stood confessed on every object, and struck me with silent admiration. – I turned to a bench under the wall, and sat so absorbed, with the charms of a cascade, so powerfully conducted in the very image of nature herself, plunging down a bed of shelving rock, and huge massy stones, that, for a long while, my attention was lost to every thing else – I strove to find out where the hand of the designer had been, but could not: – surely nothing was ever held to the eye so incomparably well executed! And if we add to its analogous accompaniments, of bold scarry grounds, rough entangled thicket, clustering trees, and sudden declivities: I cannot but be persuaded, it is altogether one of the most distinguished scenes that ever was formed by art.

. . .

A bold, artless cascade, in the very life of nature, precipitately rushes down a rugged heap of rock, huge stones, and cinders, at least one hundred and fifty paces, in a constant succession of abrupt falls, till more calm, it finds its way in a subterraneous passage under the seat into the valley below.

Ranunculus.

I really find it the greatest difficulty in the world, even to attempt a relation, that shall convey to you the least idea of its charms. – However, the intermediate ground rises steeply, studded with tall distinct oaks, and an urn extremely in character – on each side the plunging torrent, from the bottom to the top, is seen closely connected, a variety of different shrubby bushes, alders, yews, ashes, spindling among others of a more capacious bulk, the exposed roots of which grown over with moss, running over, sideways, or into the stream, have a very singular appearance; nor will you less admire the wild disorder of the numerous trees that cloath the whole glen; you will see some well grown, strong, and upright; others aslant; the trunks of many apparently growing out of the torrent; others touching it with their very branches – thus promiscuously irregular, they not only appear confusion itself, but greatly add to the strange grotesque appearance of every thing about it.'

– *Letters on the Beauties of Hagley, Envil, and the Leasowes*
by Joseph Heely (1777)

On gardening jobs for July:

'July. Leo, or the Lion.

In this Month, prune Apricots and Peaches, leaving the most likely Shoots well placed. Water young planted Trees and Layers. Let Herbs past their Season run to Seed; clip Box that grows irregular after Rain; slip Stocks, Plants and Flowers; lay Myrtles, Jessamines and other Greens. At the end of this Month, shift your Bed Offsets of Tulips, Anemonies, Ranunculus's, &c. Sow Anemony-seeds in fine sifted Earth, either in Beds or Boxes.'

– The Gentleman's, Traveller's, Husbandman's and Gardener's Pocket Companion (1751)

Repton on the avenue:

'The pleasure which the mind derives from the love of *Order*, of *Unity*, of *Antiquity*, and of *Continuity*, are in a certain degree gratified by the long perspective view of a stately avenue; even when it consists of trees in rows so far apart, that their branches do not touch: but where they grow so near as to imitate the grandeur, the gloomy shade, and almost the shelter of a Gothic Cathedral, we may add the *Comfort* and *Convenience* of such an avenue to all the other considerations of its *beauty*. A long avenue, terminated by a large old mansion, is a magnificent object, although it may not be a proper subject for a picture; but the view *from* such a mansion is perhaps among the greatest objections to an avenue, because it destroys all variety; since the same landscape would be seen from every house in the kingdom, if a view between rows of trees deserves the name of landscape.

If at the end of a long avenue be placed an obelisk, a temple, or any other *eye-trap* (as it is called), it will only catch or please the eye of ignorance or childhood. The eye of taste and experience hates compulsion, and turns with disgust from such puerile means of attracting its notice. One great mischief of an avenue is, that it divides a park, and cuts it into two distinct parts, destroying the unity of lawn; for it is hardly possible to avoid distinguishing the ground on the two sides of such an avenue into north and south park, or east and west division of the lawn.

But the greatest objection to an avenue is, that (especially in uneven ground) it often acts as a curtain drawn across the most interesting scenery: it is in undrawing this curtain at proper places that the utility of what has been called breaking an avenue consists.'

– An Enquiry into the Changes of taste in Landscape Gardening
by H. Repton (1806)

On fir trees:

'The greatest fault of modern planners is their injudicious application of fir-trees. A quick growth, and perpetual verdure have been the temptations for introducing them; but these advantages are very insufficient to justify the prevailing mode, which gives them an universal estimation. Trees of conic figure are by nature unsociable – not to be allowed a place amidst the luxuriant heads of oak, or other noblest progeny of the forest. They are sometimes beautiful as single objects – ill-suited to an extent of woodland – serviceable however to eminences of particular shape, if the size of the plantation be proportionable to the eminence, and not (as Shenstone observes, and our artists execute) like "coronets on an elephant's back". They may be loosely scattered on a wild heath: their *deep shade* may in many places be happily disposed: but when I see them in circular clumps choking up a meadow, or preposterously converted into shrubs under the branches of a forest-tree, they excite no other emotion, than contempt for the planner.'

– An Essay on Design in Gardening
by George Mason (1768)

On the summer management of grass lawns:

'To make the lawn as smooth as a carpet and to keep it free from bents and daisies, which are objectionable in the eyes of the master, the gardener must keep the lawn mown, and in dry weather these very frequent mowings with a machine do much mischief. Sometimes there is actually no grass to be cut, but simply a few daisies and other flowers, and machining a lawn to get rid of a few flowers is a great mistake. But the choice lies between the flowers remaining or a rusty-coloured lawn instead of a breadth of green. A lawn of an objectionably brown colour, be it known, is often in dry seasons the result of the grass being too closely shaven by the mowing machine or scythe.

The foregoing statements may induce some to ask, What, then, is to be done? And further, Are we to tolerate a garden of daisies? My answer is: better see Nature's flowers than to look upon a brown sun-burnt lawn that should be green. It is a too common idea that nothing but the lawn mower will keep it right, whereas if the machine is used every time a few daisies are to be seen it will make it go wrong. The proper way when there is only a very little grass to be cut is to bring the old-fashioned scythe into use, and skim the lawn over with it between 10 a.m. and noon, when the daisies are well open. The scythe will clear all before it, and the lawn will not require sweeping, as an hour or two's sunshine will render the daisies cut invisible.

This brings me to another point of importance, and this is the common mistake of carrying the cut grass off the lawn. I do not wish to convey the impression that the grass should be left to wither up at all times and all seasons; it is enough to say that discretion may be used in the matter. For the sake of the lawns, it is a great pity that there should be so much prejudice against an innovation, which, if judiciously acted upon, is capable of doing good without any extra labour. I should dispense with the grass box throughout the months of June, July, and August, in all but the very hottest summers. In positions shaded very much by trees, and low-lying wet situations, I would collect the grass all through the season, for there it might become an eyesore, but I am well sure that in many instances scattering the grass at suitable times would do a great amount of good.

The watering of lawns in dry weather can as a rule be done by those only who live in small places, or have a plentiful supply of water at command. In small gardens and where the water can be distributed through a hose, the lawn may be watered with advantage without entailing any extra amount of hard labour. Once begun, the work must be regularly continued as long as the dry weather lasts, as the watering brings into existence young roots near the surface, which speedily perish when moisture is withheld.

As regards the mowing, to the inexperienced it may appear that it does not require much skill to pass a lawn

Variety of moss.

184

mower along, but the use of the machine requires some amount of both skill and judgment. When judiciously used I have not yet seen a lawn that has not been benefited by it. When, on the other hand, it is used unskillfully, the lawns will probably be sadly disfigured by them. There are two errors that should be avoided, especially in small gardens. The first is not to purchase too large a machine; for one man, a twelve-inch or fourteen-inch mower is large enough for him to work comfortably, and he will do more work and with less fatigue with this size machine than he will with one larger. I have seen men labouring away with sixteen-inch machines, and not doing so much work as they could have done with a much smaller size, because of their being unable to push them along quickly. Such laborious work is both unnecessary and wasteful, for I know of nothing else that would so soon make a man dislike his work, and but few things will take the energy out of a man quicker than to have his strength overtaxed unnecessarily. Another source of injury to the lawn is allowing the grass to remain uncut for several days after the proper time. This is often done under the mistaken notion that time is gained by cutting the grass only at long intervals; whereas, when the grass is cut at the proper moment, the work can be done quicker, the strain upon the machine is less, and the tax upon the strength of the operator not so great; moreover, the appearance of a close-shaven lawn is better than when it has been neglected and the grass allowed to become thick and long in growth. It is a common mistake in large gardens, as well as small ones, to allow the grass to become too long; the best kept lawns are those which are cut when there is sufficient grass for the machine to do its work in a proper manner. Much will depend upon the time of year and the condition of the lawns. During the months of May and June nearly all lawns require mowing once a week, and in growing showery weather many lawns would be the better if they were machined every third day.'

– *The Beauties of Flora Display'd* by N. Swinden (1778)

Price on avenues:

'The avenue has a most striking effect, from the very circumstance of its being strait; no other figure can give that image of a grand gothic aisle with its natural columns and vaulted roof, whose general mass fills the eye, while the particular parts insensibly steal from it in a long gradation of perspective. The broad solemn shade adds a twilight calm to the whole, and makes it, above all other places, most suited to meditation. To that also its straitness contributes; for when the mind is disposed to turn inwardly on itself, any serpentine line would distract the attention . . ..

The destruction of so many of these venerable approaches, is a fatal consequence of the present excessive horror of strait lines.'

– *An Essay on the Picturesque* by Uvedale Price, 1796

On the gardens at Stowe:

'A straight road, of two miles in length, leads through an avenue of trees from Buckingham, through two Lodges, to a large Corinthian arch, or gateway, 60 feet high, and 60 feet wide, from whence appears the garden front of the House, proudly standing on the summit of a verdant slope, and encompassed by the Garden and Park. – The road turns to the right to the New Inn, where Travellers are accommodated who come to see the place, and to the entrance into the Gardens by which Strangers are admitted. – The road to the House leads through the Arch, (in which are dwelling rooms for the keeper,) into the Park, and is beautifully diversified with hill, valley, lawn, river, and a perpetual change of scene, arising from the numerous buildings intermixed with wood, and "bosomed high in

Entrance lodge.

tufted trees," which strike the eye with a most picturesque and every-varying magnificence.

. . .

The Grotto. The trees which stretch across the water, together with those which back it, and others which hang over the cavern, form a scene singularly perfect in its kind. The front of it is composed of the roughest stones and spars. The inside is finished with a variety of shells, spars, fossils, petrifactions, and stalactites. At the upper end is a circular recess, in which are two basons of white marble: in the upper is placed a fine marble Statue of Venus rising from her bath, and from this the water falls into the lower bason, from whence it is conveyed under the floor to the front, where it falls into the river through the lower cavern.'

— *Stowe: A Description of the House and Gardens*
by Thomas Medland (1817)

Creating serpentine walks:

'SERPENTINE WALKS, of gravel or grass, being such as are conducted in various windings, sweeps, and turnings, in a natural imitation, and to afford a greater source of variety, by exhibiting new and different objects at every different turning; and to give an opportunity of a more considerable scope of walking . . ..

In forming serpentine walks, the sweeps should not be too frequent and sudden, nor ought the turnings be too stiff or all of regular dimensions, in some places let the windings advance, gradual and easy, in other let the sweeps be bold, sometimes considerably long, and sometimes short and sudden, in different parts, so as at every turning it may discover different varieties in the plantation, &c. which is one particular merit in serpentine walks, as well as to afford more extensive walking than in walks perfectly straight; for serpentine walks may be so varied by winding them different ways, as to furnish considerable walking within a small compass of ground.'

— *The Young Gardener's Best Companion* by S. Fullmer (1786)

Gilpin on Studley:

Studley in North Yorkshire includes an impressive water garden and pleasure ground which was laid out *c.*1718 to 1730 by John Aislabie, the owner of the house. Aislabie was able to devote money and energy to the remodelling of the grounds after his involvement in the South Sea Bubble caused him to lose his seat in parliament.

'The most improved part of the gardens at Studley, and what is chiefly shewn to strangers, is a valley, nearly circular, surrounded by high woody grounds, which slope gently into it in various directions. The circumference of the higher grounds includes about one hundred and fifty acres; the area, at the bottom, consists of eight. The higher parts present many openings into the country. The lower, of course, are more confined; but might afford many pleasing woody scenes, and solitary retreats. A considerable stream runs through the valley: and on the banks of this stream, in another valley, contiguous to the circular one, stand the ruin of Fountain's

A View in the Garden of Mr Aislabie Esq. at Studley in Yorkshire.

Engraving of Studley, 1776.

abbey; the grandest, and most beautiful, except perhaps those of Glastonbury, which the kingdom can produce.

The idea, which such a scene suggests, is that of retirement – the habitation of cheerful solitude. Every object points it out; all tending to sooth and amuse; but not to rouse and transport; like the great scenes of nature.

. . .

Instead of these ideas, which the scenes of Studley naturally suggest, the whole is a vain ostentation of expence; a mere *Timon's villa*; decorated by a taste debauched in it's conceptions, and puerile in it's execution. Not only the reigning idea of the place is forgotten; but all the great master-strokes of nature, in every shape are effaced . . ..

What a lovely scene might a person of pure taste have made at Studley, with one tenth part of the expence, which hath been laid out in deforming it.

. . .

On the whole, it is hard to say, whether nature has done more to embellish the scenes of Studley; or art to deform them. Much indeed is below criticism. But even, where the rules of genuine taste have been adopted, they are for the most part unhappily misapplied. In the point of the opening views, for instance, few of the openings here are simple, and natural. The artifice is apparent. The marks of the sheers, and hatchet, are conspicuous in them all. Whereas half the beauty of a thing consists in the easiness of it's introduction. Bring in your story awkwardly; and it offends. It is thus in a view. The eye roving at large in quest of objects, cannot bear prescription. Every thing forced upon it, disgusts; and when it is apparent, that the view is *contrived*; the effect is *lost*.

. . .

Such was the general idea of this beautiful valley, and of the ruins which adorned it, before they fell into the hands of the present proprietor. Long had he wished to draw them within the circle of his improvements: but some difficulties of law withstood. At length they were removed; and the time came (which every lover of picturesque beauty must lament) when the legal possession of this beautiful scene was yielded to him; and his busy hands were let loose upon it. He found it indeed somewhat ruder, than even picturesque beauty required; and a little might have been well done. But his improvements have had no bounds. He has pared away all the bold roughness, and freedom of the scene, and given every part a trim polish.

A few fragments lying scattered around the body of a ruin are *proper*, and *picturesque*. They are proper because they account for what is defaced: and they are picturesque because they unite the principal pile with the ground; on which union the beauty of composition, in a good measure, depends. But here they were thought rough and unsightly; and feel sacrifice to neatness.

. . .

But the *restoration* of parts is not enough: *ornaments* must be added: and such incongruous ornaments, as disgraced the scene, are disgracing also the *ruin*. The monk's garden is turned into a trim parterre, and planted with flowering shrubs: a view is opened, through the great window, to some ridiculous figure, (I know not what; Ann Bolein, I think, they called it) that is placed in the valley.'

— *Observations on the Mountains and Lakes of Cumberland and Westmoreland* by William Gilpin (1786)

On fountains:

'BASONS, *or* Fountains, *&c.* which serve either for the Ornament or Use of Gardens, are made in divers Forms, some round, some oblong, or oval, others square, octangular, &c. but their most common Form is circular; and if the Ground will permit, the larger they are, the better: And when they exceed in Size, they are call'd pieces of Water, Canals, Mirrors, Fish-ponds, Pools, and Reservoirs.

In making these, Care ought to be taken to avoid both the Extremes, and not to make them either too big or too little; that a Water-work may not take up the best Part of a small Spot of Ground; nor to make too little a Bason in a large Spot. This must depend intirely on the Judgment of the Designer of the Garden.

Some would have the Size of a *Bason* to be proportion'd to the *Jet' d'Eau*, that the Water thrown up in the Air, may not, by being blown by the Air, be carry'd beyond the Edge of the *Bason*, but all fall down without wetting the Walk.

Others again say, That let the Spout rise to never so little a Height, tho' the *Bason* be large, the Wind blow the Water to a great Distance, and tho' it be very disagreeable to see a slender Stream in a large *Bason*, and a large high stream in a small *Bason*; and tho' there should be as great an Agreement as is possible between the Stream of the Spout and the *Bason*; yet no precise Proportion can be fix'd between

Drooping fountains.

the Size of *Basons* and their Spouts; because that depends
upon the Place where the *Fountain* is situated.'

– *The Gardeners Dictionary* by Philip Miller (1737)

On gardening jobs for August:

'August. Virgo, or the Virgin sign.

Prune off superfluous Branches and Shoots of the second Spring; pluck up Suckers from about the Root; inoculate
early, if at all in this Month. Sow Colliflowers and Cabbages
for Winter plants; as also Corn, Sallad, Marygolds, Lettuce,
Carrots, Parsnips, Spinage, Onions, Endive, Angelica,
Scurvy-grass, Lark's-heel, Columbines, Fox Gloves,
Hollyocks, and such plants as endure Winter. Transplant
such Lettuce as you would have abide all Winter; pull up ripe
Onions, Garlick, &c. gather such Seeds as are ripe, and clip
such Herbs before the Full of the Moon, an handful high.
Sow Purslain, Chervil, &c. Make Summer Cyder and Perry,
and gather seeds from such shrubs that are thorough ripe.'

– *The Gentleman's, Traveller's, Husbandman's and*
Gardener's Pocket Companion (1751)

On Blenheim Palace:

'The gardens are spacious and agreeable: They originally consisted of about 100 acres, but the present Duke has made large additions, and elegant improvements. The noble descent to the water on the south and west, covered with flowering shrubs, and embellished with other natural beauties, will hardly be paralleled by any Garden in this Kingdom.

About the middle of the grand approach, is a magnificent BRIDGE, chiefly consisting of one Arch, in the style of the Rialto at Venice; the water above the Bridge, is formed into a spacious Lake, which covers the whole extent of a capacious valley, surrounded by an artificial declivity of a prodigious depth. On the other side it forms a noble serpentine river.

The PARK is between ten and eleven miles in circumference, and contains many delightful scenes. The lover of rural variety will be entertained here with every circumstance of beauty, which he can expect from diversified nature; from hill and valley, water and woods.'

— *The New Oxford Guide* by a Gentleman of Oxford (1759)

A letter on the beauties of Hagley:

'This stately mansion stands upon easy rising ground, in the midst of a rich and capacious lawn: except on the North side, where for convenience, are the offices and kitchen garden: but these, by very elegant shrubbery, filled with a variety of evergreens, and verged with luxuriant full grown limes, and other trees, totally conceal every offensive object, from any point of view throughout the whole park . . ..

The park from hence exhibits a landscape that would do honour to the pencil of a Poussin*: – an inexpressible glow of the sublime and beautiful, in all the fullness of their powers. – Immediately opposite, happily distanced, on the brow of a finely polished lawn, stands a tall and light column, embosomed by a sweeping grove of pines and elms, falling down the hill, and seemingly connected with the trees that surround a small gothic church, within about a hundred paces from the foot. Large oaks single, and others in groups, from hence grace another swelling lawn, diversified

---

* Nicolas Poussin (1594–1665) was one of the foremost artists of the French Baroque. He painted many large scenes with a religious or mythological theme, which often included great swathes of beautifully rendered landscape.

with patches of fern, extending itself in fine inequalities to a different and loftier compartment of a wood, that gradually diminishes to a light, airy grove, yet affording over its branches a precipitate slant of the green hills of Clent – bold, high and picturesque.

. . .

No vista surely has ever held to the eye with such advantages to please! – With what attention, and even transport does not almost every stranger look on the clear lake before him! – on the majestic spreading trees that paint its steep and bold swelling sides, nature dropped, bending their horizontal arms, and dipping down to the curling wave! What does he not even *feel*, when he marks the playing cascade, gush from the shrub-grown rocky banks, in foaming plunge, down the close embosomed vale! – when he casts his eyes on those variegated shrubby crossings, and slants of lawn above – on green rising knole at the extremity of view, covered sometimes with the browsing deer, and crowned with a rotundo, in perfect character, and in perfect beauty! While round him the melody of thrush, the blackbird, and other different warblers, give their wild, and cheerful notes, to

Varieties of iris.

make it still more delightful! – He stands in rapture – he gazes – contemplates – and with reluctance, leaves the elysian bower!

. . .

Hagely has a pre-eminence over most of the pleasure grounds I am acquainted with – it not only affords a multiplicity of scenes, but every one rises somewhat different in character, though all of them perfectly relative; and what adds still more to its glory, is, that you always conclude the present can never be rivalled by another, till another appears, and, with its beauty and unexpected novelty, effaces the impression the former has made upon you.'

– Letters on the Beauties of Hagley, Envil, and the Leasowes
by Joseph Heely (1777)

On creating variety in planting:

'Variety is produced in two ways: by varying the disposition and distance of trees of the same kind relatively to one another, which may be said to produce simple variety; by varying the disposition and distance of trees of the same kind with shrubs principally of one kind, which may be said to produce variety joined to intricacy; and by the use of trees and shrubs of many different kinds, which may be said to produce harmony. The addition of intricacy to variety, by the use of shrubs, is equally easy, since it is nothing more than a repetition of the mode using trees without shrubs; but, where harmony is to be introduced by the use of trees and shrubs of many kinds, some knowledge of botany and of the art of plant culture is required, as well as a knowledge of art.'

– The Suburban Gardener and Villa Companion
by J. C. Loudon (1838)

On borders:

'BORDERS: The Use of these in a Garden is to bound and inclose Parterres, to prevent them being injur'd by walking in them: These are commonly render'd very ornamental by means of the Flowers, Shrubs, Yews, &c. that are planted in them.

These ought to be laid with a Rising in the Middle, because if they are flat, they are not agreeable to the Eye.

As for their Breadth, five or six Feet are often allow'd for the largest, and four for the lesser.

Borders are of four Sorts; and those are the most common that are continu'd about Parterres without any Interruption, and are wrought with a sharp Rising in the Middle like an Ass's Back, and planted with Yews, Shrubs and Flowers.

The second sort of *Borders* are such as are cut into Compartiments at convenient Distances by small Passages; and being also rais'd in the Middle, as before-mention'd, are likewise set off with Shrubs.

The third Sort are such as are laid even and flat, without Flowers, having only a Verge of Grass in the Middle, being edg'd with two small Paths rak'd smooth and sanded: These are sometimes garnish'd with flowering Shrubs and Yews, or with Vases and Flower-pots plac'd regularly along the Middle of the Verge or Grass.

The fourth Sort are quite plain, and are only sanded, as in the *Parterres* of *Orangery*, and are fill'd with Cases rang'd in a regular Order along those *Borders* which are edg'd with Box on the Sides next to the Walks, and on the other, with the Verges and Grass-work on the *Parterre*: Sometimes a Yew is planted between each Case, which makes the Border appear richer, and the *Parterres* handsomer during the Winter-Season.'

– *The Gardeners Dictionary* by Philip Miller (1737)

Walpole on views and prospects:

'Sir Henry Englefield was one of the first improvers on the new style, and selected with singular taste that chief beauty of all gardens, prospect and fortunate points of view: we tired of all the painter's art when it wants these finishing touches. The fairest scenes, that depend on themselves alone, weary when often seen. The Doric portico, the Palladian bridge, the Gothic ruin, the Chinese pagoda, that surprize the stranger, soon lose their charms to their surfeited master. The lake that floats the valley is still more lifeless, and its lord seldom enjoys his expence but when he shows it to a visitor. But the ornament whose merit soonest fades, is the hermitage or scene adapted to contemplation. It is almost comic to set aside a quarter of one's garden to be melancholy in. Prospect, animated prospect, is the theatre that will always be the most frequented.'

— *The History of the Modern Taste in Gardening*
by Horace Walpole (1780)

On cultivating a collection of grasses in pleasure-grounds or flower-gardens:

'A COLLECTION of the different species of grasses arranged in a distinct compartment of the pleasure-ground or flower-garden will be found to constitute one of its most interesting features. It has been justly observed by Sir James Edward Smith in his English Flora, that the grasses afford more sustenance to man and to the large animals than all the rest of the vegetable kingdom together; their herbage so perpetually springing, and so tenacious of life, accommodated in one instance or other to almost every climate, soil, and situation, affords nature her most welcome clothing, and to the cultivator of the soil his chief riches . . ..

The grasses constitute one of the most perfect natural orders of plants, and although humble, and until lately, over-looked by the general observer, consist of upwards of a thousand perfectly distinct species, distinguished from each other by their specific botanical characters . . ..

The flowers of grasses are perfect, and are remarkable for the simplicity and elegance which pervades their whole structure; they will be found to want only examination to excite our admiration that so slender and

Chervil.

simple a structure should be productive of such important ends, and capable of receiving upwards of a thousand clear specific shades of variation without in the lest affecting its primary essential family character.'

– 'On Cultivating a Collection of Grasses in Pleasure-grounds or Flower-gardens' by Mr. George Sinclair, Nurseryman, from *The Gardener's Magazine* by J. C. Loudon (1826)

Repton on Woburn:

Repton delivered his designs for Woburn's gardens to the 6th Duke of Bedford in 1805, though some of his designs were adopted for the pleasure ground, many others were never realised. Repton famously bound his designs in red leather and thus they became known as his 'Red Books'. Repton would detail his ideas, providing beautiful watercolours of the plans, often utilising a flap to reveal a 'before' and 'after' image of what he envisaged.

'Thus the pleasure-ground at Woburn requires to be enriched and furnished like its palace, where good taste is every where conspicuous. It is not by the breadth or length of the walk that greatness of character in garden scenery can ever be supported; it is rather by diversity, and the succession of interesting objects. In this part of a great place we may venture to extract pleasure from *variety*, from *contrast*, and even from *novelty*, without endangering the character of *greatness*.

. . .

I must not here omit the full tribute of applause to that part of the drive at Woburn, in which evergreens alone prevail: it is a circumstance of grandeur, of variety, of novelty; and, I may add, of winter comfort, that I never saw adopted in any other place on so magnificent a scale. The contrast of passing from a wood of deciduous trees to a wood of evergreens, must be felt by the most heedless observer; and the same sort of pleasure, though in a weaker degree, would be felt in the course of a drive, if the trees of different kinds were collected in small groups or masses by themselves instead of being blended indiscriminately.'

> *– An Enquiry into the Changes of taste in Landscape Gardening*
> by H. Repton (1806)

On straight lines:

'It is not easy to account for the fondness of former times for straight-lined avenues to their houses: straight-lined walks through their woods; and, in short, every kind of straight line; where the foot is to travel over, what the eye has done before. This circumstance is one objection. Another, somewhat of the same kind, is the repetition of the same object, tree after tree, for a length of way together. A third is, that this identity is purchased by the loss of variety, which the natural country supplies every where, in a greater or less degree. To stand still and survey such avenues, may afford some slender satisfaction, through the change derived from perspective; but to move on continually and find no change of scene on the least attendant on our change of place, must give actual pain to a person of taste.'

— *The Works in Verse and Prose of*
William Shenstone (1777, 5th ed.)

A description of Brown's working method:

Unlike other great gardeners of the era, such as Humphry Repton and J. C. Loudon, Capability Brown wrote no books on his methods and theories of landscape design, leaving his work to speak for itself. Fortunately, we do have this glimpse of his working methods which was provided by an encounter with the writer Hannah More in 1782. More wrote to her sister in the summer of 1782 about conversing with Brown in the gardens of Hampton Court Palace:

'Never was such delicious weather! I passed two hours in the garden the other day as if it had been April with my friend Mr. Brown. I took a very agreeable lecture from him in his art, and he promised to give me taste by inoculation. He illustrates everything he says about gardening by some literary or grammatical allusion. He told me he compared his art to literary composition. "Now *there*," said he, pointing his finger, "I make a comma, and there," pointing to another spot, "where a more decided turn is proper, I make a colon; at another part, where an interruption is desirable to break the view, a parenthesis; now a full stop, and then I begin another subject."'

— W. Roberts and H. More, *Memoirs of the Life and Correspondence of Mrs. Hannah More*, vol. 1 (London: 1835), p. 267.

On garden design for a country seat:

'Let us now examine the general Idea of a good Design, and how a Country Seat may be best distributed; so that Profit and Pleasure may be well mix-d together, that those Methods that have made Gardening and Planting burden-some and expensive, may in some measure be remov'd, and that the Designs themselves may be more rural, natural, more easy and less expensive, both in the making, and keeping, and in Reality more intermixt both in Respect to Profit and Pleasure, than any Designs or Methods that have been yet taken.

For to speak the Truth of this matter, most of those that have pretended to give Designs in Gardening, have confin'd their thoughts too narrowly into a sort of fine Sett Gardening, which can't be denied to be curious in its kind: But it is withal so very Expensive in the making (and which is of almost an eternal Duration the keeping) that very few Gentlemen can, or at least care to alienate so much Land, and so much Yearly Revenues, towards the maintenance of those prodigious Gardens, which are made in some Parts of England. Whilst other Gentlemen of very good Genius's, and Dispositions seem (and that with a great deal of Reason) to esteem them as too stiff and formal, and (tho' very great in their way) not capable of giving so great satisfaction to the eye of the Beholder, as the more beautiful, tho' less elaborate Works of Nature; justly complaining that our English Gardeners instead of imitating Nature, love to deviate from it as much as possible, and esteem nothing worth minding that is not set off with the utmost Art imaginable. And, that if their Plants are not Pyramids or Conical, they are by no means valuable. When in truth the loose Tresses of a Tree or Plant, that is easily fann'd by every gentle Breeze of Air, and the natural tho' unpolisht dress of a beautiful Field, Lawn or Meadow (a little trimm'd, and the exorbitant Luxury of their Branches retrencht, cut off and redress'd; and when their even clean Walks of Gravel, Sand, or any other material For-Walk spread over) are much more entertaining than the utmost exactitude of the most finishst Parterre, and the curiousest Interlacings of Box Work and Embroidery.'

– *Ichnographia Rustica* by Stephen Switzer (1718)

On Chatsworth:

'On leaving the sculpture gallery, we pass into the orangery, where scattered among orange-trees, rhododendrons, and some magnificent exotics, are a number of fine statues and a singular curiosity in the shape of an enormous single

crystal*, weighing several hun-
dredweights. From the orangery
we enter the gardens and make
a tour of them under the guidance of one of the gardeners, of
whom some threescore and ten are
here in constant employment. A
walk of a few minutes brings us to
the front of the celebrated cascade,

Bastard service berries.

which at first view recalls to remembrance the grand cascade at St. Cloud as it existed before the late misfortunes of
France. Like that, it consists of a series of flights of steps,
though it is on a smaller scale. The entire structure reclines
on the slope of a hill; the volume of water descends from
a classic temple adorned with dolphins, naiads, sea-lions,
and other marine monsters, through the mouths and urns
of which, as well as from other concealed vomitories, the
fountain streams forth, and covering the broad surface of
the channel dashes headlong down the steep, disappears
at the bottom among masses of rock, and flows thence
by an underground route into the River Derwent. A very
different kind of waterwork is an artificial tree which we

---

* This crystal is over a metre tall and was found in the Simplon Pass in
Switzerland. It was gifted to Duchess Georgiana, who was a keen collec-
tor of minerals, in 1793. Today it sits in the South Sketch.

come upon soon after quitting the cascade, and which is so contrived that, at a touch from the attendant it spouts forth from every branch and twig a shower of close rain upon persons who happen to be beneath it or too near it, and who must retreat pretty quickly if they would escape a thorough drenching. There are, however, in the grounds, waterworks of a far more important description; such are the jets and fountains, one of which sends its column of water near a hundred feet high, and another which plays only on special festive occasions, and hurls its jet to more than double that height, or about as high as the monument in London. In connection with the waterworks should be mentioned the rockworks, with which in fact they are in a manner combined. These consist of rocky precipices of towering height, and picturesque ravines, all of them being artificially constructed (some of them even copied from actual natural scenes), and yet so natural in appearance that no one not informed of the fact could suppose them to be other than what they seem.

The great wonder of the gardens, however, is the conservatory, erected by the late Sir Joseph Paxton, and which was the precursor of the Crystal Palace of 1851. It is in the form of a parallelogram, and covers more than an acre of ground; it is a most superb object to look at, and vast though it is in size, one might almost imagine it a living creature just alighted on the spot from some far-off wonderland. For its construction were required 70,000 square feet of glass, and the sash-bars, if laid end on end, would extend for forty miles. We do not much relish the tropical heat within, though we can but linger over the spectacle of the magnificent exotics it contains, and of which both hemispheres have furnished their proportions. For the convenience of royal visitors there is a carriage-drive round the interior.

In the course of our horticultural promenade we pass various other objects of interest, of which we can barely mention a few. One is the Emperor Fountain, a memorial of the Czar Nicholas, who visited Chatsworth in 1844; others are trees planted by royal personages, as an oak planted by Queen Victoria, when princess, in 1832; a chestnut planted by her mother, Duchess of Kent; a sycamore planted by the late Prince Consort in 1843, etc., etc. With the Italian garden, which shows like a miniature park, and might serve for a living illustrations of the scene of Boccaccio's Decameron, we close our hasty survey of the grounds.'

– Extracted from an article in 'The Leisure hour: a family journal of instruction and recreation' edited by James Macauley (5 September 1874)

On gardening jobs for September:

'September. Libra, or the Ballance.

Gather your ripe Winter-Fruit, be sure in dry Weather. You may yet sow Radishes, Lettuce, Spinage and Winter-Herbs. Transplant most part of Eating and physical Herbs, Artichokes, Asparagus Roots, Strawberries, &c. As the Weather alters about Michaelmas, in fair Weather (but not in a foggy Day) retire your favourite Greens, and choicest plants being dry into the Conservatory. When the cold comes on, set such plants as will not endure the House, into the Earth, two or three Inches below the surface, and under a southern Exposure, covered and cloathed with Hay for their security against the Cold of the Night; but open them in sun-shiny-Days, and again in favourable warm showers.'

— *The Gentleman's, Traveller's, Husbandman's and Gardener's Pocket Companion* (1751)

On the character of the ground:

'Ground should first be considered with an eye to it's peculiar character: whether it be grand, the savage, the sprightly, the melancholy, the horrid, or the beautiful. As one or other of these characters prevail, one may somewhat strengthen it's effect, by allowing every part some denomination, and then supporting it's title by suitable appendages – For instance, The lover's walk may have assignation seats, with proper mottoes – Urns to faithful lovers – Trophies, garlands, &c. by means of art.'

> – *The Works in Verse and Prose of*
> *William Shenstone* (1777, 5th ed.)

Monthly calendar for the flower garden:

'JANUARY. – Sow and place in pots hardy annuals, such as sweet peas, lupins, &c. In open weather plant bulbous roots.

FEBRUARY. – Sow anemones, sow hardy annuals in borders if the weather opens, sow also hardy biennials, and put in your remaining bulbs; sow dahlias and place the tubers in hot beds or under glass in a border to break buds for slipping; sow hardy perennials, plant suckers, slips, and partings of roots; by the end of the month complete the

Poppy anemone and star aneomone.

planting of flowering shrubs, sow also polyanthuses, balsams, and cockscombs, and other tender annuals may be sown by affording protection when requisite.

MARCH. – Sow tender annuals in pots and borders to remain, sow biennials, carnations, and polyanthuses, and annuals generally.

APRIL. – Sow hollyhocks, pinks, and all your remaining annuals or biennials, in mild weather prick out those sown in February, and plant out the biennials sown last spring.

MAY. – Greenhouse plants may be now removed into the open border: take up and store bulbous roots generally when the leaves decay.

JUNE. – Sow biennials and perennials for next year if omitted last month. Take up bulbs and prick our seedlings.

JULY. – Plant heartsease slips, and transplant perennials and biennials, lay down your carnations.

AUGUST. – Sow anemones, sow ten-week stocks, sow also tulips and other bulbous-rooted flower seeds: carnations may still be laid.

SEPTEMBER. – Sow hardy annuals for next year, and also bulbous roots for early blooming.

OCTOBER. – Sow hardy annuals, plant anemones and bulbs, cut carnation layers to be planted in pots; begin to take up dahlias as the flowers cease.

NOVEMBER. – Plant anemones if not done last month, finish planting bulbous roots, and take up dahlias after the first frost: plant ranunculuses if omitted last month.

DECEMBER. – Defend anemones, auriculas, and carnations in severe weather; tulips should also be defended in bad weather. Fibrous-rooted perennials and biennials to be divided and planted: bulbs may still be planted in mild weather.'

– Gardener's Manual for the Fruit, Flower and
Kitchen Garden (1859)

The Rotunda at Stowe:

'NOT far from hence a majestic Edifice rises, called, The Rotunda: There is not a Piece of Stone-work in the whole Garden that makes a more beautiful Figure than this, in point of Perspective; it is an airy Building, by Sir JOHN VANBRUGH. The Dome is supported on Ten Ionic

Columns; and, in the Centre, standing on a circular Pedestal, is a *Venus a Medicis*: It stands on a gentle Rise, and a beautiful View of the Queen's Theatre, NELSON's Seat, and its fine Canal, the Belvidere, Pyramid, and first Prospect of the Lake.

. . .

From this Place we have a View of Part of the Lake, the great Lawn, and several other Buildings, presenting themselves alternately as we turn ourselves round: On one Side you have an Opening, laid out with all the Embellishments of Art; on the other, a spacious Theatre: Here you behold an Area, watered by a clear Canal, where wantonly sport a vast Number of Swans, Wild ducks, and Peacocks, &c. Her late Majesty's is the principal Figure in the Scene . . ..

AND around her a merry Company of Nymphs and Swains, enjoying themselves in the Shade. This is absolutely a most charming Prospect. And then, on the opposite Side, what a beautiful Contrast! For which we are almost solely obliged to Nature. The Lawn is formed by that Semicircle of Trees in a very grand Theatre. The Point of Sight is centered in a beautiful manner by the Pyramid, which appears to great Advantage amongst those venerable Oaks; two or three other Buildings half hid amongst the Trees, which come in for a Share in the Prospect, and add much to the Beauty of it. Nor do I think this other View inferior to it: That Variety of Shades among the Trees: the Lake spread so elegantly amongst them, and glittering here and there through the Bushes; with the Temple of VENUS, as a Termination to the View. Here is a Visto likewise, very happily terminated by the Canal. There is another close View likewise, toward's NELSON's Seat. In short, here is a Variety of very elegant Prospects, centered in this Point, which make up some very beautiful Landscapes.'

– *The Beauties of Stow* by George Bickham (1753)

On novelty in the garden:

'There seem however to be some objects, which afford a pleasure not reducible to either of the foregoing heads. A ruin, for instance, may be neither new to us, nor majestic, nor beautiful, yet afford that pleasing melancholy which proceeds from a reflexion on decayed magnificence. For this reason, an able gardener should avail himself of objects, perhaps, not very striking; if they serve to connect ideas, that convey reflexions of the pleasing kind.

Objects should indeed be less calculated to strike the immediate eye, than the judgment or well-formed imagination; as in painting.

It is no objection to the pleasure of novelty, that it makes an ugly object more disagreeable. It is enough that it produces a superiority betwixt things in other respects equal. It seems, on some occasions, to go even further. Are there not broken rocks and rugged grounds, to which we can hardly attribute either beauty or grandeur; and yet when introduced near an extent of lawn, impart a pleasure equal to more shapely scenes? Thus a series of lawns, though ever so beautiful, may satiate and cloy, unless the eye passes to them from wilder scenes; and then they acquire the grace of novelty.'

> – *The Works in Verse and Prose of*
> *William Shenstone* (1777, 5th ed.)

On gardenesque style:

'Where the gardenesque style of imitating nature is to be employed, the trees, shrubs, and herbaceous plants must be separated; and, instead of being grouped together as in forest scenery (where two trees, or a tree and a shrub, often appear to spring from the same root, and this root is accompanied by large rampant herbs), every gardenesque group must consist of trees which do not touch each other, and which only become groups by being as near together as is practicable without touching, and being apart from larger masses, or from single trees or rows of trees. It is not meant by this, that in the gardenesque style the trees composing the group should all be equally distant from one another; for in that case they would not form a whole, which the word group always implies. On the contrary, though all the trees in a gardenesque group ought to be so far separated from each other as not to touch, yet the degrees of separation may be as different as the designer chooses, provided the idea of a group is not lost sight of . . ..

In planting, thinning, and pruning, in order to produce gardenesque effect, the beauty of every individual tree and shrub, as a single object, is to be taken into consideration, as well as the beauty of the mass: while in planting, thinning, and pruning for picturesque effect, the beauty of individual trees and shrubs is of little consequence; because no tree or shrub, in a picturesque plantation or scene, should stand isolated, and each should be considered as merely forming part of a group or mass. In a picturesque imitation of nature, the trees and shrubs, when planted should be scattered over the ground in the most irregular manner; both in their disposition with reference to their immediate effects

Dewberry.

as plants, and with reference to their future effect as trees and shrubs. In some places trees should prevail, in others shrubs; in some parts of the plantation should be thick, in others it should be thin; two or three trees, or a tree and a shrub, ought often to be planted in one hole, and this more especially on lawns. Where, on the contrary, trees and shrubs are to be scattered in the gardenesque manner, every one should stand singly; as in the geometrical manner they should stand in regular lines, or in some regular figure. In the gardenesque, there may be single trees and single shrubs; but there can be no such thing as a single tree in the picturesque. Every tree, in the picturesque style of laying out grounds, must always be grouped with something else, if it should be merely a shrub, a twiner, or a tuft of grass or other plants at its root. In the gardenesque, the beauty of the tree consists in its own individual perfections, which are fully developed in consequence of the isolated manner in which it has been grown; in the picturesque, the beauty of a tree or shrub, as of every other object in the landscape, consists in its fitness to group with other objects. Now, the fitness of one object to group with another evidently does not consist in the perfection of the form of that object, but rather in that imperfection which requires another object to render it complete.'

– *The Suburban Gardener and Villa Companion*
by J. C. Loudon (1838)

Whately on Stowe:

'This is the character of the gardens at Stowe; for there the views into the country are only circumstances subordinate to the scenes; and the principal advantage of the situation is the variety of the ground within the enclosure. The house stands on the brow of a gentle ascent; part of the gardens lie on the declivity, and spread over the bottom beyond it; this eminence is separated by a broad winding valley from another which is higher and steeper; and the descents of both are broken by large dips and hollows, sloping down the sides of the hills. The whole space is divided into a number of scenes, each distinguished with taste and fancy; and the changes are so frequent, so sudden, and complete, that the same ideas are never continued or repeated to satiety.

These gardens were begun when regularity was in fashion; and the original boundary is still preserved, on account of its magnificence; for round the whole circuit of between three and four miles, is carried a very broad gravel walk, planted with rows of trees, and open either to the park or the country; a deep-sunk fence attends it all the way, and comprehends a space of near four hundred acres. But in the interior scenes of the garden, few traces of regularity appear; where it yet remains in the plantations, it is generally disguised; every symptom almost of formality is obliterated from the ground; and an octagon basin in the bottom, is now converted into an irregular piece of water, which receives on one hand two beautiful streams, and falls on the other down a cascade into a lake.

. . .

On the right of the lawn, but concealed from the house, is a perfectly garden scene, called the queen's amphitheatre, where art is avowed, though formality is avoided; the fore ground is scooped into a gentle hollow; the plantations on the sides, though but just rescued from regularity, yet in style are contracted to each other; they are, on one hand, chiefly thickets, standing out from a wood; on the other, they are open groves, through which a glimpse of the water is visible: at the end of the hollow, on a little knole, quite detached from all appendages, is placed an open Ionic rotunda; beyond it a large lawn slopes across the view; a pyramid stands on the brow; the queen's pillar in a recess on the descent; and all the three buildings being evidently intended for ornament alone, are peculiarly adapted to a garden scene, yet their number does not render it gay; the dusky hue of the pyramid, the retired situation of the queen's pillar, and the solitary appearance of the rotunda, give it an air of gravity; it is encompassed with wood; and all external views are excluded; even the opening into the lawn is but an opening into an enclosure.

. . .

Immediately above the alder grove is the principal eminence in the gardens; it is divided by a great dip into two pinnacles, upon one of which is a large Gothic building; the space before this structure is an extensive lawn; the ground on one side falls immediately into the dip; and the trees which border the lawn, sinking with the ground, the house rises above them, and fills the interval: the vast pile seems to be still larger than it is; for it is thrown into perspective, and between and above the heads of the trees, the upper story, the porticoes, the turrets, and ballustrades, and all the slated roofs appear in a noble con-fusion: on the other side of the Gothic building, the ground slopes down a long continued declivity into a bottom, which seems to be perfectly irriguous; divers streams wander about it in several directions; the conflux of that which runs from the Elysian fields with another below it, is full in sight; and a plain wooden bridge is thrown over the latter, and

Crocus versicolor.

evidently designed for a passage, imposes an air of reality on the river; beyond it is one of the Doric porticoes which front the house; but now it is alone; it stands on a little bank above the water, and is seen under some trees at a distance before it; thus grouped, and thus accompanied, it is a happy incident, concurring with many other circumstances to distinguish this landskip by a character of chearfulness and amenity.'

— Observations on Modern Gardening
by Thomas Whately (1770)

On fences near the house:

'If there be any part of my practice liable to the accusation of often advising the same thing at different places, it will be true in all that relates to my partiality for a *Terrace* as a fence near the house. Twenty years have, at length, by degrees accomplished that line of demarcation betwixt art and nature, which I have found so much difficulty in establishing, viz. a visible and decided fence betwixt the mown pleasure-ground and the pastured lawn; betwixt the garden and the park; betwixt the ground allotted to the pleasure of man, and that to the use of cattle . . ..

The necessity of a fence to protect the house from cattle seems to have been doubted by the followers of Brown, who generally used the Ha! Ha! Supposing that the fence ought to be invisible. On the contrary, it cannot surely be disputed, that some fence should actually exist between a garden and a pasture; for if it is invisible, we must either suppose a cattle to be admitted into a garden, or flowers planted in a field; both equally absurd . . ..

A magnificent Palace ought not (like many that might be mentioned) to stand in a grass field, exposed to cattle, which are apt to take shelter near the building, and even to enter it, where there is no fence to prevent them; but a terrace or balustrade marks the line of separation. The inside of the inclosure may be decorated with flowers; and we feel a degree of security for them and for ourselves, by knowing that there is a sufficient fence to protect both.'

– *Fragments on the Theory and Practice of Landscape Gardening*
by Humphry Repton (1816)

Remarks on the effect of the cedar of Lebanon, in landscape:

'THE cedar of Lebanon assumes a very romantic and imposing appearance, and from its frequent mention in sacred history, is ever associated with ideas of grandeur and architectural magnificence. There is even something architectural in its form; the thick upright stem, supporting the horizontal branches, in a great measure accord with the pillars and copings of buildings . . ..

Thus it may be inferred that cedars should always be the accompaniment of palaces, public buildings, and superior residences, though they are seldom met with so situated.

The finest I have seen are at Blenheim; but even there they are not much contrasted with the architecture, but are spread generally throughout the whole of the gardens; and they appeared to me in great measure lost from being so mixed up with other trees and shrubs; however, they serve to maintain the character of grandeur which belongs to this place . . ..

The form and character to the cedar is not suited to any thing on a small scale, or that betrays want of effect in its architectural features, or in the disposition of the ground: thus one would not place them in the centre of a home meadow, or arable field, where oaks and elms are sometimes met with, having a very good effect; nor should they appear where the scenery is either domestic, or homely, or tame. Nothing annoys me more than to find a cedar, a cypress, or other stately tree, contrasting itself with hay-stacks, and dove-cotes, in the garden of some old farm-house . . ..

The cedar will not bear to be planted too thickly, or too close together; it should be placed by twos and threes in conspicuous situations, such as on small mounds, or by the side of water, next bridges or temples; sometimes on lawns, or rising grounds that command extensive prospects, where it may serve as a fore-ground; but they must not be made too common by being seen at every turn: too many of them will always destroy their effect.'

> – 'Remarks on the Effect of the Cedar of Lebanon, in
> Landscape' by Mr John Thompson. Article from
> *The Gardener's Magazine* by J. C. Loudon (1826)

On the order of planting trees in the pleasure ground:

'The disposition or order of planting the various trees and shrubs in the pleasure ground, should be in different arrangements, as formerly observed, to effect as great a diversity as possible in the general plan, by forming the following different divisions and compartments, or such of them as the

Planting trees: clump, thicket and groups.

scope of ground admits, viz. Lawns—Shrubberies—Tree plantations—Wilderness—Groves—Thickets—Clumps—Avenues—Shady walks—Wood walks—Recesses—Glades, or Opens—Bosquets—Ranges of Trees—Dotting trees singly—Groups of trees—Hedge-rows of trees—Hedges—Arbours—Labyrinths or mazes—Rookeries: Also to adorn garden buildings, as Temples—Grottos—Rock-work—Ruins—Hermitages: Likewise Waters, &c.'

– *The Young Gardener's Best Companion* by S. Fullmer (1786)

On laying out a suburban garden:

'However paradoxical it may seem, it is nevertheless true, that the difficulties of building, planting, and gardening, on a small scale, so as completely to attain the objects in view, are greater than on a large one. This will be found acknowledged by the late eminent landscape-gardener, Mr. Repton, in various parts of his works; and it is also well known to every architect, and to every gentleman's gardener who has been accustomed to lay out grounds. There is scarcely an architect who does not find it much easier to satisfy himself in devising a design for a mansion, than one for a cottage residence; or a landscape-gardener, who would not have more confidence of success in laying out and planting a park of a thousand acres, than a ground plot of half an acre. The difficulty, in the case of small places, arises from the deep consideration required to produce the greatest possible result from very limited means. In building or planting on a large scale, the means are generally ample; and, if not unlimited, they are, at least, frequently indefinite: the results obtained are, therefore, generally considerable, and such as to afford ample enjoyment to the possessor. Should they fail of this, however, his wealth and his resources will enable him to alter, amend, and improve, till he has succeeded to his wishes; or, should he ultimately not succeed, will prevent him from being ruined by the attempt. The builder of a small house, on the contrary, whether it is for his own occupation, or for that of another, undertakes a task of great moral responsibility; since the result may either be inadequate to the means employed, and thus time and money which can ill be spared may be thrown away; or the expense may be greater than was desired, or could be afforded by the party, and might thus blight his fortune, and, consequently, mar his prospects of happiness.'

– *The Suburban Gardener and Villa Companion*
by J. C. Loudon (1838)

On avenues:

'AVENUES, are Walks or Entrances leading to a Place, and in Gardening, are Walks planted with Rows of Trees, made in the Front-end of the Garden, leading to the Front of an House, or to a Garden Gate, to a Highway gate or Wood, to terminate in a Prospect.

As to such *Avenues* that lead to an House, they ought to be as wide as the whole Breadth of the Front, and if they be wider they are better.

And as for such *Avenues* to Woods or Prospects, &c. they ought not to be less than sixty foot in Breadth; and because such Walks are a long time before they are shady, it will be convenient to plant another Row on each Side, rather than to lose the Stateliness that the main Walk will afford in Time by being broad, where any thing of a Prospect is to be gained.

And as to the Distance one from another, they should not be planted nearer to one another than thirty-five or forty

Feet, especially if the Trees are any thing of a spreading kind; and the Same Distance if they are for a regular Grove.

As to the Trees proper for planting Avenues, they may be the *English Elm*, the *Lime Tree*, the *Horse Chesnut*, the *common Chesnut*, the *Beach* [sic], and the *Abele*.'

— *The Gardeners Dictionary* by Philip Miller (1737)

On gardening jobs for October:

'October. Scorpio, or the Scorpion.

In this Month it is proper to set Fruit-stones; set them three Inches deep, and the sharp End uppermost, and cover them with straw; also you may sow this Month Genoa Lettuce, which with small Care will be good Sallading all Winter; cover them with Bell-Glasses in hard Weather.'

— *The Gentleman's, Traveller's, Husbandman's and Gardener's Pocket Companion* (1751)

On the Belvidere at Stowe:

'But let us move forwards towards yon Cubico-pyramidical Building, called the BELVIDERE: the whole Use of which is to contribute to the different Vista's that terminate there, through a Thousand charming Allies. It looks like a substantial one: However, it terminates this Terras exceeding well. The Ascent up to it, too, has good Effect; and so has the Field on the Right, its Beauties: How it strikes you at first Sight! It is designed, like a Glass of Bitters before Dinner, to quicken your Appetite for the elegant Entertainment that is to follow: For my Part, I find it a very great Relief to my Eye, to take it from those Grand Objects, and cast it for a few Minutes upon such a rural Scene.'

– *The Beauties of Stow* by George Bickham (1753)

Definitions of tree planting:

'Wood, as a general term, comprehends all trees and shrubs in whatever disposition; but it is specifically applied in a more limited sense, and in that sense I shall now use it.

Every plantation must be either a *wood*, a *grove*, a *clump*, or a *single tree*.

A wood is composed both of trees and underwood, covering a considerable space. A grove consists of trees without underwood; a clump differs from either only in extent; it may be either close or open; when close, it is sometimes called a *thicket*; when open, a *groupe of trees*; but both are equally clumps, whatever be the shape or situation.'

— Observations on Modern Gardening
by Thomas Whately (1770)

Remarks on the effect of the Lombardy poplar in park scenery:

'THE Lombardy poplar is a tree, which, as applied to the science of arboriculture, is capable of producing not only the most noble and striking, but the greatest variety of effect; and perhaps, there is no tree which has the misfortune to be in general so injudiciously planted. I have, therefore, sent you a few remarks founded upon the study of landscape composition, in which I do not intend to say any thing of the bad or good qualities of the poplar, but merely to consider it as a tall conical mass of foliage, which becomes of great import, when contrasted with the more useful and valuable round headed trees.

First then, it is a known pictorial rule, that all horizontal lines should be balanced and supported by perpendicular ones: – thus, the effect of a bridge or via-duct would be greatly increased by the assistance of poplars . . ..

The poplar, therefore, would be advantageously planted wherever there is a continuance of horizontal lines; but they should be so arranged as to form part of those lines, to seem to grow out of them, rather than to break or contrast with them in too abrupt a manner. In the case of a stable or other agricultural building, where the principal mass extends in length rather than height, it would be wrong to plant them exactly before it, but they should be at the sides or behind . . ..

The poplar should also appear in all plantations and belts that are made with a view to picturesque effect, but more particularly, they should be introduced in a sparing but judicious manner in all pleasure-grounds; and they are quite indispensable in the formation of such groups as are intended to convey an impression of that grand and classical simplicity, which is, or should be, the first object in all ornamental planting.'

> – 'Remarks on the Effect of the Lombardy Poplar in Park Scenery' by Mr. John Tompson, landsurveyor and pictorial draughtsman. Article from *The Gardener's Magazine* by J. C. Loudon (1826)

$\mathcal{O}n$ water:

'In considering the subjects of gardening, ground and wood first present themselves; water is the next, which, though not absolutely necessary to a beautiful composition, yet occurs so often, and is so capital a feature, that it is always regretted when wanting; and no large place can be supposed, a little spot can hardly be imagined, in which it may not be agreeable; it accommodates itself to every situation; is the most interesting object in a landscape, and the happiest circumstance in a retired recess; captivates the eye at a distance, invites approach, and is delightful when near; it refreshes an open exposure; it animates a shade; chears the dreariness of a waste, and enriches the most crouded view: in form, in style, and in extent, may be made equal to the greatest compositions, or adapted to the least: it may spread in calm expanse, to sooth the tranquillity of a peaceful scene; or hurrying along a devious course, add splendour to a gay, and extravagance to a romantic, situation. So various are the characters which water can assume, that there is scarcely

Cowslip.

an idea in which it may not concur, or an impression which it cannot enforce: a deep stagnated pool, dank and dark with shades which it dimly reflects, befits the feat of melancholy; even a river, if it be sunk between two dismal banks, and dull both in motion and colour, is like a hollow eye which deadens the countenance; and over a sluggard, silent stream, creeping heavily along all together, hangs a gloom, which no art can dissipate, nor even the sun-shine disperse. A gently murmuring rill, clear and shallow, just gurgling, just dimpling, imposes silence, suits with solitude, and leads to meditation: a brisker current, which wantons in little eddies over a bright sandy bottom, or babbles among pebbles, spreads chearfulness all around: a greater rapidity, and more agitation, to a certain degree are animating; but in excess, instead of wakening, they alarm the senses; the roar and the rage of a torrent, its force, its violence, its impetuosity, tend to inspire terror; that terror, which, whether cause or effect, is so nearly allied to sublimity.'

– *Observations on Modern Gardening*
by Thomas Whately (1770)

Repton on moving objects:

'A scene, however beautiful in itself, will soon lose its interest, unless it is enlivened by moving objects; and from the shape of the ground near the houses, there is another material use in having cattle to feed the lawn in view of the windows. The eye forms a very inaccurate judgment of extent, especially in looking down a hill, unless there be some standard by which it can be measured; bushes and trees are of such various sizes, that it is impossible to use them as a measure of distance; but the size of a horse, a sheep, or a cow, varies so little, and is so familiar to us, that we immediately judge of their distance from their apparent diminution, according to the distance at which they are placed; and as they occasionally change their situation, they break that surface over which the eye passes, without observing it, to the first object it meets to rest upon.'

– An Enquiry into the Changes of taste in Landscape Gardening
by H. Repton (1806)

Price on the intricacy of varied ground:

'What most delights us in the intricacy of varied ground, of swelling knolls, and of vallies between them, retiring from the sight in different directions amidst trees or thickets, is, that it leads the eye (according to Hogarth's expression) a kind of wanton chace; this is what he calls the *beauty* of intricacy, and is that which distinguishes what is produced by soft winding shapes, from more sudden and quickly-varying kind, which arises from broken and rugged forms. All this wanton chace, as well as the effects of more wild and picturesque intricacy, are immediately checked by any circular plantation; which never appears to retire from the eye, and lose itself in the distance, nor ever admits of partial concealments. Whatever varieties of hills and dales there may be, such a plantation must stiffly cut across them, and the undulations, and what in seamen's language may be called the *trending* of the ground, cannot in that case be humoured; nor can its playful character be marked by that style of planting, which at once points out, and adds to its beautiful intricacy.'

– *An Essay on the Picturesque* by Uvedale Price, 1796

On designing a pleasure garden:

'The Area of a handsom Garden may take up thirty or forty Acres, not more. And as for the Disposition and Distribution of this Garden, the following Directions may be observ'd.

1st, There ought always to be a Descent from the House to the Garden not fewer than three Steps. This Elevation of the Building will make it more dry and wholesome: Also, from the Head of these Steps there will be a Prospect or View of a great Part of the Garden.

In a fine Garden, the first Thing that should present it self to the Sight, is a Parterre, which should be next to the House, whether in the Front, or on the Sides, as well upon account of the Opening it affords to the House, as for the Beauty with which it constantly entertains the Sight from all the Windows on that Side of the House.

As for the Parterres, they must be furnish'd with such Works as will improve and set them off; and they being low and flat, do necessarily require something that is rais'd, as Groves and Palisades. But in this Case, Regards must be had to the Situation of the Place; and before planting, it ought to be observ'd whether the Prospect that Way be agreeable; for the sides of the Parterre should be kept intirely open, making Use of Quarters of Grass, and other flat Works, in order to make the best of the View: And also it ought to be carefully avoided, not to shut it up with Groves, unless they be planted in Quincunx Order, or open'd with low Hedge-rows; so as not to hinder the Eye from piercing through the Trees, and so discovering Beauties of the Prospect on every side.

If there be no Visto, but on the contrary, there be a Mountain, Hill, Forest, or Wood, that, being near, will intercept the Prospect; or if there be some Village adjoining too near, the houses of which are no agreeable Sight, then you may edge the Parterre with Palisades and Groves, to screen those disagreeable Objects from the View.

Groves make the Chief of a *Garden*, being great Ornaments to all the rest of its Parts; so that there cannot be too many of them planted, if the Places design'd for them don't take up those of the Kitchen and Fruit-Garden which are very necessary for a House, and should always be plac'd near the Stabling.

. . .

It would also be very proper to plant some Groves of Ever-greens, that may afford the Pleasure of seeing a Wood always verdant in Winter, when the other Trees and Plants are depriv'd of their Ornaments; and also to plant some squares of them to be a Diversity from the other Woods.

It is also usual to adorn the Head of a Parterre with Basons, water-works; and beyond it, with a circular Line of Palisades or Wood-work cut into a Goose-foot, leading into the great Walks, and to fill the Space between the Bason and the Palisade with small Pieces of Embroidery or Grass-work, set off with Yews, Vases and Flower-pots.

. . .

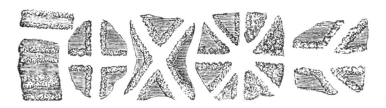

Avenue; double avenue; Greek cross; martyr's cross; star; and goose foot.

The principal Walk must be in the Front of the House, and another Walk ought to be cross it at right Angles: If they be double, and very wide, the Sides should be turfed next to the Borders, and at the ends they may be terminated by a Fossee [fosse, a trench or ditch], to continue the View.

. . .

When the great Lines and chief Walks are laid out, and the Parterres and Works about the Sides and Head of them are dispos'd so as is most suitable to the Ground, then the rest of the Garden is to be furnish'd with many different Designs, as *Tall Groves, Close Walks, Quincuxes, Galleries* and *Halls of Verdure, Green Arbours, Labyrinths, Bowling-greens*, and *Amphitheatres*, adorn'd with *Fountains, Canals, Figures*, &c. Which sort of Works distinguish a Garden well, and do also greatly contribute to the rendering of it magnificent.'

– *The Gardeners Dictionary* by Philip Miller (1737)

On the construction of a moderate hot-bed for tender annual flowers:

'A week or more before the seeds are intended to be sown, prepare some fresh horse-dung, the quantity in proportion to the number of lights intended; two cart loads to a three-light box will be full sufficient, or somewhat less may do. Near the spot destined for the bed (which should be well sheltered behind from cold bleak winds,) let this dung be shook up in a heap, lightly and evenly, so as to mix equal parts of short and long together: in this heap it should lay to ferment for three, four, or more days, according to the freshness of the dung; the heap should be drawn in narrow at the top, to keep off heavy rains, or snow, which would chill it more, being flat. When it is come to a regular heat, proceed to make the bed, the size of which should first

Crocus varieties.

be marked out on the ground, eight or more inches wider each way than the extremity of the box. As it is making, let the longest of the dung be laid about a foot within the edge of ground marked out, still filling up the middle, and keeping it evenly worked up with equal parts of short and long together, gently pressing and beating it down with the back of the fork, to find if any light hollow places yield to the pressure, which if any, should be kept filled, that every part may be equally solid, or otherways it will settle uneven, so that in some places the plants will rise (perhaps burn) while others will not have heat sufficient to vegetate. When the bed is finished, let the glasses be put on, observing to give air sufficient to let off the steam, and when the heat is temperate, and the steam somewhat abated, level the surface very even, and cover it with fine sifted mould five inches deep.'

– *The Beauties of Flora Display'd* by N. Swinden (1778)

To prevent slugs, or snails, from destroying a crop, or any favourite plants in the garden:

'It has been common to surround the plant, or the border, with lime; but this soon loses its effect, especially if there comes rain: but a *certain* preventative is, to spread coarsely powdered glass, an inch broad, and *all round* the border, or plant. This they never can get over, and therefore all that might come from a distance, will be guarded against. It will be proper to look over the borders, for two or three evenings after this is done, that if any slugs were under the earth, within the circle of glass, they may be taken and destroyed. If the bed be dry, water it; and about an hour after dark, go with a lantern and look over it. Thus it will be soon freed, and no others can come into it.'

— *Valuable Secrets relative to Gardening and Agriculture Now Made Known* by Jedediah Simmons (1795)

On wildernesses:

'WILDERNESSES, if rightly situated, artfully contriv'd, and judiciously planted, are the greatest Ornaments to a fine Garden: But it is rare to see these so well executed in Gardens, as to affords the Owner due Pleasure (especially if he is a Person of an elegant Taste), for either they are so situated as to hinder a distant Prospect, or else are not judiciously planted: The latter of which is scarce ever to be found in any of our most magnificent Gardens, very few of their Designers ever studying the natural Growth of Plants, so as to place them in such manner, that they may not obstruct the Sight from the several Parts of the Plantation which are presented to the View . . ..

The usual Method of contriving Wilderness is, to divide the whole Compass of Ground either into Squares, Angles, Circles, or other Figures, making the Walks correspondent to them; planting the Sides of the Walks with Hedges of Lime, Elm, Hornbeam, &c. and the Quarters within are planted with various kinds of Trees promiscuously without Order. But this can no means be esteem'd a judicious Method, because hereby there will be a great Expence in keeping the Hedges of a large Wilderness in good Order, which instead of being beautiful, are rather the Reverse; for as these Parts of a Garden should, in a great measure, be design'd from Nature, so whatever has the stiff Appearance of Art, does by no means correspond therewith.'

– *The Gardeners Dictionary* by Philip Miller (1737)

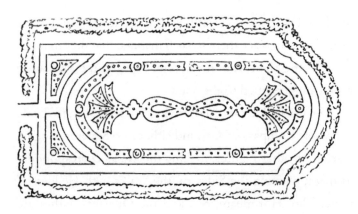

Layout of a flower garden.

In praise of Stowe:

'While a Taste for Painting, Music, Architecture, and other polite Arts, in some Measure, prevailed amongst us, our Gardens, for the most part, were laid out in so formal, aukward, and wretched a Manner, that they were really a Scandal to the Genius of the Nation: A Man of Taste was shocked whenever he set his Foot into them. But STOW, it is to be hoped, may work some Reformation. I would have our Country Squires flock hither two or three Times a Year, by way of Improvement; and, after they have looked about them a little, return home with new Notions, and begin to see the Absurdity of their clipped Yews, their Box-wood Borders, their flourished Parterres, and their lofty Brick-walls.'

– *The Beauties of Stow* by George Bickham (1753)

On gardening jobs for November:

'November. Saggitary, or the Archer.

Now trench and fit Ground for Artichokes, and plant Trees for standards and Walls. Also lay in your Cellars, Carrots, Turnips, Parsnips, Cabbages, and Colliflowers for Seed, to be transplanted in the Spring. Now also take up Potatoes for Winter's spending.'

— *The Gentleman's, Traveller's, Husbandman's and Gardener's Pocket Companion* (1751)

On the ornamented cottage garden:

'Neatness and simplicity ought to mark the style of this rational retreat. Ostentation and show should be cautiously avoided; even elegance should not be *attempted*: though it may not be *hid*, if it offer itself spontaneously.

Nothing, however, should appear vulgar, nor should simplicity be pared down to baldness; every thing whimsical or expensive ought to be studiously avoided: — chasteness and frugality should appear in every part.

Near the house, a *studied neatness* may take place; but, at a distance, negligence should rather be the characteristic.

If a taste for botany lead to a collection of native shrubs and flowers, a shrubbery will be requisite; but, in this, every thing should be native. A gaudy exotic ought not to be admitted; nor should the lawn be kept close shaven; its flowers should be permitted to blow; and the herbage, when mown, ought to be carried off, and applied to some useful purpose.

. . .

In fine, the ORNAMENTED COTTAGE ought to exhibit cultivated Nature in the first stage of refinement. It ranks next above the farm-house. The plain garb of rusticity may be set off to advantage; but the studied dress of the artist ought not to appear.'

– Planting and Ornamental Gardening; A Practical Treatise
by William Marshall (1785)

The pleasure ground:

'For since the Pleasure of a Garden depends on the variety of its Parts, 'tis therefore that we should well consider of their Dispositions, so as to have a continued Series of Harmonious Objects, that will present new and delightful Scenes to our View at every Step we take, which regular Gardens are incapable of doing. Nor is there any Thing more shocking than a stiff regular Garden; where after we have seen one quarter thereof, the very same is repeated in all the remaining Parts, so that we are tired, instead of being further entertain'd with something new as expected.'

– *New Principles of Gardening* by Batty Langley (1728)

On elegance and Painshill:

'The elegance and propriety of rural designs seem greatly to depend on a nice distinction between *contrast* and *incongruity*. To define the exact limits of each in every instance is a task next to impossible; but the judicious eye will immediately discover the difference in objects presented before it. In general we may observe, that confusion arises from crowding together into *one* scene, what would be infinitely pleasing

A Scene in the Gardens of Pain's Hill.

Engraving of Paine's Hill gardens, 1776.

in *two* successively. At Paine's Hill the banks of the lake are admirably contrasted by the wild rusticity on the other side of the arch. As the scenes are separated from each other by a sufficient interposition of thicket, the effect of surprise is created by the contrast: had they been less distinct, incongruity must have been striking.'

– An Essay on Design in Gardening
by George Mason (1768)

On Chatsworth:

'This extensive part presents a great variety of aspect, from the most graceful undulating hill and swelling eminence, interspersed with plantations, beautiful lawns and pleasure grounds to the bold rugged cliff and lofty mountain, well watered and richly wooded, including an area of about 11 miles in circumference, stocked with about two thousand head of deer, sheep and cattle in vast numbers, and kept in the finest possible order.

. . .

The massive and richly ornamented square pile of the old house, with its rusticated base, beautiful Ionic fluted columns – pilasters, – ornamented frieze, – and pediment, (the arms of the Devonshire family most admirably sculptured in stone within the tympanum,) all surmounted with an open balustrade, divided into sections, and adorned with urns, vases, and statues, – the simple, quiet beauty of the *new wing* in the Grecian style, with its elegant offices projecting considerably forwards, about midway, judiciously breaking its vast extent, the magnificent temple soaring aloft, with its open columns as a beautiful finish to the northern wing, and a striking counterpart to the massive pile, to the south, – the fine platform on which it stands, studded at intervals with graceful trees, which relieve the broad mass of exquisite masonry of a rich buff colour, with veins of a reddish tinge, giving the whole structure a golden hue, – the elegant terraces extending nearly 1200 feet, and flower garden, with its "*jet d'eau*" in front, – the expansive river and

Pine varieties.

fine grounds beneath, with groups of fallow deer and cattle reposing under the ample shade of beech or chestnut, – all this backed with hanging woods of great magnificence and beauty, form an exquisite picture and scarcely to be equalled in the three kingdoms! On a fine sunny day it is truly sublime, and it need scarcely be observed that we stood for a while to contemplate a scene so enchanting – a scene which a century ago could not have been dreamed of as likely to exist amongst healthy mountains and the wilds of the Peak. But it exhibits a splendid specimen of the enrichment of art, and the capability of a world, however sterile and forbidding in its natural aspect, of being converted, by persevering industry and judicious management, into a very Paradise.'

– Description of Buxton, Chatsworth and Castleton
by William Adam (1847)

How to plant a great variety of trees and shrubs:

'If the sorts are mixed together indiscriminately, the result is left to chance; if they are mixed together as equally as possible, then the result must necessarily be monotony, by the same number of kinds appearing in every part of the plantation; and, if each kind is kept in a group or mass by itself, there will be a risk of want of connexion, and, consequently, of unity in the general result. In what ways are all these difficulties to be overcome? Chiefly, we should say, by keeping each sort by itself, and placing all those sorts nearest each other which are most alike; avoiding all formality in the outlines of the spaces allotted to each sort; and allowing these spaces to indent or ramify into one another. For this purpose, a knowledge of the natural system of botany is of the greatest use to the landscape-gardener; since it teaches him that all those trees and shrubs that belong to the same natural family, order, or tribe, admit of being brought together in the same group. The chief difficulty therefore, will be in joining or connecting the groups together; and, here a general rule may be given. This is, that, when the groups have a near general resemblance to each other, such as those of *Quercus* with *Ulmus*, or *Crategus* with *Pyrus*, then the union may be comparatively abrupt; that is, with a slight intermixture of the trees of both groups at the points where they join. But, when the groups are very dissimilar, such as when the pine and fur tribe adjoin deciduous trees, the union must be very gradual, by means of numerous indentations and ramifications of the one group into the other. For example, suppose it were desirable to join a large mass of different species of oak with a large mass of different species of pine; then, adjoining some of the evergreen oaks in the one group, place one or two pines, which grow in large and compact forms; and against some of the half-evergreen oaks, such as the Fulham or old Lucombe oak, place one or two pines of comparatively slender growth. In like manner, in the opposite group, evergreen and half-evergreen oaks may be planted among the pines, so as to form the extreme points of the oak group in that direction; and, as the one group approaches the other, not only evergreens and half-evergreens, but deciduous species, in equal numbers, may be introduced. In all this, care must be taken to avid regular progression, and every thing like formality.'

— *The Suburban Gardener and Villa Companion*
by J. C. Loudon (1838)

On the wild garden at Tew Park:

Great Tew Park in Oxfordshire includes a section which was laid out under the guidance of Humphry Repton who provided advice on its situation and design. Subsequently, from 1808, the park was managed by J. C. Loudon, where he laid out the north and south drives and added many trees to the park and surrounding village.

Flower garden layout.

'Tew Park will long be interesting, from the fact that it was there J. C. Loudon practised agriculture before he began writing the works which were such a marked addition to the horticultural literature of England. The Grove there is a plantation of fine trees, bordering a wide sweep of grass, which varies in width. This grove, unlike much of the rest of the ground, does not vary in surface, or but very little, so that one of the greatest aids is absent. Originally this now pleasant grove was a dense wood, with Gout-weed mainly on the ground, and troublesome flies in the air. A few years ago the formation of a wild garden was determined upon, and the first operation was the thinning of the wood; light and moving air were let into it, and weak or overcrowded trees removed. This, so far, was a gain, quite apart from the flowers that were in good time to replace the few common weeds that occupied the ground. Of these the unattractive Gout-weed was the most abundant, and the first thing to do was to dig it up. It was found that by deeply digging the ground, and sowing the wood Forget-me-not in its place, this weed disappeared. Who would not exchange foul weeds for Lillies of the Valley and Wood Forget-me-nots! The effect of broad sheets of this Wood Forget-me-not (Myosotis sylvatica) beyond, and seen above the long waving Grass gradually receding under the trees, was very beautiful; now (June) its beauty is not so marked as earlier, when the colour was fuller from the plants being more compact; but one charm of the wild garden is that the very changes of plants from what may be thought their most perfect state, may be in itself the source of new pleasure instead of a warning, such as so often occurs in the garden, that we must cut them down or replace them.'

– *The Wild Garden* by W. Robinson (1883)

On gardening jobs for December:

'December. Capricorn, or the Goat.

In this Month prune Standard-Trees and Wall-Fruit trees, Vines and Stocks for Grafting; set early Pease and Beans, &c.'

— *The Gentleman's, Traveller's, Husbandman's and Gardener's Pocket Companion* (1751)

Mason on Brown:

Poet William Mason (1724–97) was a keen gardener and wrote the four-part poem *The English Garden*. As an admirer of Capability Brown's work, he was chosen to pen Brown's epitaph, which can still be seen in Fenstanton church in Cambridgeshire:

'You sons of elegance, who truly taste, the simple charms which genuine art supplies, come from the sylvan scenes his genius graced, and offer here your tributary sighs, but know that more than genius slumbers here, virtues were his which art's best powers transcend, come, ye superior train who these revere, and weep the Christian, husband, father, friend.'

— William Mason, 1783

A poem in praise of the English Garden:

'Yet in this wild disorder Art presides,
Designs, corrects, and regulates the whole,
Herself the while unseen. No cedar broad
Drops his dark curtain where a distant scene
Demands distinction. Here the thin abele
Of lofty bole, and bare, the smooth-stem'd beech,
Or slender alder, give our eye free space
Beneath their boughs to catch each lessening charm
Ev'n to the far horizon's azure bound.

Nor will that sov'reign Arbitress admit,
Where'er her nod decrees a mass of shade,
Plants of unequal size, discordant kind,
Or rul'd by Foliation's different laws;
But for that needful purpose those prefers
Whose hues are friendly, whose coeval leaves
The earliest open, and the latest fade.

Nor will she, scorning truth and taste, devote
To strange, and alien soils, her seedling stems;
Fix the dank fallow on the mountain's brow,

Or, to the moss-grown margin of the lake,
Bid the dry pine descend. From Nature's laws
She draws her own: Nature and she are one.'

— *The English Garden: A Poem in Four Books*
by W. Burgh, 1794

Loudon on the joys of gardening:

'One of the greatest of all the sources of enjoyment result-
ing from the possession of a garden is, the endless variety
which it produces, either by the perpetual progress of vege-
tation which is going forward in it to maturity, dormancy or
decay, or by the almost innumerable kinds of plants which
may be raised in even the smallest garden. Even the same
trees, grown in the same garden, are undergoing perpetual
changes throughout the year; and trees change also, in every
succeeding year, relatively to that which is past; because they
become larger and larger as they advance in age, and acquire
more of their characteristic and mature forms.'

— *The Suburban Gardener and Villa Companion*
by J. C. Loudon (1838)

A final word:

'. . . the best and most general Rules that (in words) I can possibly lay down, are to endeavour to follow and improve the Advantages of Nature, and not to strain her and her due Bounds.'

– *Ichnographia Rustica* by Stephen Switzer (1718)

INDEX